Social Issues
in Literature

Freedom of Thought
in Jerome Lawrence
and Robert Edwin Lee's
Inherit the Wind

Other Books in the Social Issues in Literature Series:

Social Issues
in Literature

Freedom of Thought in Jerome Lawrence and Robert Edwin Lee's *Inherit the Wind*

Candice Mancini, Book Editor

GREENHAVEN PRESS
A part of Gale, Cengage Learning

Detroit • New York • San Francisco • New Haven, Conn • Waterville, Maine • London

GALE
CENGAGE Learning·

Christine Nasso, *Publisher*
Elizabeth Des Chenes, *Managing Editor*

© 2011 Greenhaven Press, a part of Gale, Cengage Learning

Gale and Greenhaven Press are registered trademarks used herein under license.

For more information, contact:
Greenhaven Press
27500 Drake Rd.
Farmington Hills, MI 48331-3535
Or you can visit our Internet site at gale.cengage.com

For product information and technology assistance, contact us at

Gale Customer Support, 1-800-877-4253
For permission to use material from this text or product, submit all requests online at www.cengage.com/permissions

Further permissions questions can be emailed to permissionrequest@cengage.com

Articles in Greenhaven Press anthologies are often edited for length to meet page requirements. In addition, original titles of these works are changed to clearly present the main thesis and to explicitly indicate the author's opinion. Every effort is made to ensure that Greenhaven Press accurately reflects the original intent of the authors. Every effort has been made to trace the owners of copyrighted material.

Cover image © Photos 12/Alamy.

LIBRARY OF CONGRESS CATALOGING-IN-PUBLICATION DATA

Freedom of thought in Jerome Lawrence and Robert Edwin Lee's Inherit the wind / Candice Mancini, book editor.
    p. cm. -- (Social issues in literature)
    Includes bibliographical references and index.
    ISBN 978-0-7377-5014-0 -- ISBN 978-0-7377-5015-7 (pbk.)
    1. Lawrence, Jerome, 1915-2004 Inherit the wind. 2. Lee, Robert Edwin, 1918-1994 Inherit the wind. 3. Freedom of speech in literature. I. Mancini, Candice.
    PS3523.A934I54 2010
    812'.54--dc22
                                                        2010012986

Printed in the United States of America
1 2 3 4 5 6 7 14 13 12 11 10

Contents

Chapter 1: Background on Jerome Lawrence and Robert Edwin Lee

Chapter 2: *Inherit the Wind* and Freedom of Thought

Chapter 3: Contemporary Perspectives on Freedom of Thought

Introduction

In creating *Inherit the Wind*, Jerome Lawrence and Robert Edwin Lee intended to criticize McCarthyism—the government policy of accusing Americans of subversive, Communist activities that was led by Senator Joseph McCarthy during the 1950s—yet it is the play's theme of evolution versus creationism that strikes audiences most today. The evolution debate was not as controversial in 1955, when the play premiered, as it is today. The fact that *Inherit the Wind* premiered in Dallas, Texas, to a receptive audience was evidence of this. Still, premiering in Dallas seemed risky at the time. As Lawrence and Lee's agent warned Dallas director Margo Johnson: "Margo, you don't want to do this play. Everybody will—will crucify you down there in the Bible Belt." Johnson's instincts, however, proved accurate: the play was not only a success in Dallas but also moved on to Broadway and became one of the most widely produced plays ever.

"*Inherit the Wind* is not history," said the playwrights in their introduction to the play. "The events which took place in Dayton, Tennessee, during the scorching July of 1925 are clearly the genesis of this play. It has, however, an exodus entirely its own." Nonetheless, *Inherit the Wind* undoubtedly shaped the interpretation of history, and in particular, the historical event of the *Scopes* trial and its aftermath. Some critics of evolution claim that the impact of *Inherit the Wind* has hurt their cause because the play's depiction of antievolutionists as ignorant and backward-thinking has been stamped in the minds of audiences. Yet many pro-evolutionists view the play's effects as more damaging to their side, claiming that the success of the play has given them a false sense of security that their view is unassailable. Either way, since *Inherit the Wind*'s premiere, the dispute about teaching evolution in the classroom has become increasingly heated in American society. In this way, the play is timelier now than it was in 1955.

Those professing alternatives to evolution generally fall under two categories: creationists and intelligent-design theorists. Creationists argue that God created the world and all life within it, as detailed in the biblical book of Genesis. Intelligent design, according to its proponents, offers an alternative explanation of creation, claiming that, instead of life forming as a result of natural selection (as evolutionists argue), life resulted from a supernatural, intelligent design. Although intelligent design theorists do not specifically identify God as the designer, intelligent design theory was posited by creationists.

Evolutionists argue that although evolution is theory, not fact, it differs from creationism and intelligent design in that as a theory of science, evolution has undergone, time and again, the intense scrutiny of the scientific method. This increases its validity, even if the theory does not explain everything or have all of the answers to humankind's questions about its existence on earth. Albert Einstein's statement, "We still do not know one-thousandth of one percent of what nature has revealed to us," remains applicable. In contrast, the Web site of the Creation-Science Research Center provides a different justification for the center's beliefs: "We believe in creation, first of all, not because of scientific evidence, but because of our faith in Jesus Christ . . . Creation is by definition a divine miracle, an act of God which is outside of and above the physical laws He has established in the world. Therefore, scientists who believe in creation do not try to devise theories to explain how God was created, for human beings cannot understand how God was created."

Thus far, neither creationism nor intelligent design has made its way into the classroom, to be taught alongside the theory of evolution, but efforts to get them there continue to grow. The issue is a matter of ongoing debate within school boards, the court system, and the American political arena.

The selections in this volume offer various perspectives on how this debate has been influenced by the play *Inherit the Wind*.

Chronology

1915

Jerome Lawrence is born on July 14 in Cleveland, Ohio, to Samuel Lawrence, the owner of a printing company, and Sarah Rogen Lawrence, a poet.

1918

Robert Edwin Lee is born on October 15 in Elyria, Ohio, to Claire Melvin Lee, an engineer, and Elvira Taft Lee, a teacher.

1933

Lawrence graduates from Glenville High School in Cleveland.

1935

Lee graduates from Elyria High School.

1934–1942

Lee studies for one year at Northwestern University near Chicago in 1934. He then transfers to Ohio Wesleyan University in Delaware, Ohio, where he is a student from 1935 to 1937. While at Wesleyan, he works as a technician at a local observatory. In 1937, he leaves school and his observatory job to take a directing job at a Cleveland radio station. After this, he studies for one year at Cleveland's Western Reserve University. Shortly after, he leaves school again to work at an ad agency in New York City. He never earns a bachelor's degree.

Lawrence graduates Phi Beta Kappa from Ohio State University in 1937; he attends graduate school at the University of California at Los Angeles (UCLA) from 1937 to 1939. While in California, Lawrence works as a radio station continuity editor and as a CBS senior staff writer. He works for CBS until 1942.

1942

Lawrence and Lee form a writing partnership, for radio, television, theater, and film. Their first collaboration, "Inside a Kid's Head," is produced for *Columbia Workshop*.

Lawrence and Lee enter the armed forces, where they cowrite and produce programs for the Armed Forces Radio Service. They write numerous radio programs and dramas, including *Mail Call, Command Performance*, and *The World We're Fighting For*.

1945–1947

After leaving military service, Lawrence and Lee continue to publish radio shows and dramas, including *Request Performance, Favorite Story*, and *The Frank Sinatra Show*.

1948

On January 29, Lawrence and Lee's play *Look, Ma, I'm Dancin'!* premieres at Adelphi Theatre in New York. They continue to produce radio shows and dramas.

Lee marries radio actress Janet Waldo.

1948–1954

Lawrence and Lee produce, direct, and write 299 broadcasts of the weekly radio series *The Railroad Hour*, in addition to other radio and television programs.

1955

On January 10, Lawrence and Lee's play *Inherit the Wind* premieres at Theatre '55 in Dallas, Texas. After garnering good reviews, the play opens on Broadway on April 21 at the National Theatre.

1956

On June 13, Lawrence and Lee's play *Shangri-La* premieres at Winter Garden Theatre in New York; *Auntie Mame* premieres at Broadhurst Theatre in New York. Several plays follow in subsequent years.

1965

Lawrence and Lee's play *Inherit the Wind* is broadcast on *Hallmark Hall of Fame* on NBC-TV.

1961

Lawrence and Lee establish the Margo Jones Award as a memorial to the Dallas producer of *Inherit the Wind*.

1966

Lawrence's play *Live Spelled Backwards* premieres at the Beverly Hills Playhouse in Los Angeles, California; Lawrence and Lee's musical *Mame* premieres at Winter Garden Theatre in New York.

1970

Lawrence and Lee's *The Night Thoreau Spent in Jail* premieres at the Ohio State University.

1973

Lee's *Ten Days That Shook the World* premieres at the Freud Playhouse at the University of California at Los Angeles.

1978

Lawrence and Lee's play *First Monday in October* premieres as their final play performed on Broadway.

1981

First Monday in October is adapted into a motion picture.

1990–1993

Lawrence and Lee's *Whisper in the Mind* premieres at Arizona State University, Tempe, in 1990 (a revised version premieres at Missouri Repertory Theatre, Kansas City, in 1994).

In 1990, Lawrence and Lee are named to the American Theatre Hall of Fame and are named Fellows of the American Theatre at the Kennedy Center, Washington, D.C. The writing pair receives other prestigious awards in the theatre in their lifetimes, including the Donaldson Award, the Ohioana Award, Variety Critics Poll, two Peabody Awards, and the Lifetime Achievement Award from the American Theatre Association.

1994
On July 8, Lee dies of cancer in Los Angeles, at the age of seventy-five.

2004
On February 29, Lawrence dies in Malibu, California, following a stroke, at the age of eighty-eight.

Background on Jerome Lawrence and Robert Edwin Lee

The Lives of Jerome Lawrence and Robert Edwin Lee

Alan Woods

Alan Woods is an associate professor at the Ohio State University's Department of Theatre and the director of the university's Jerome Lawrence and Robert E. Lee Theatre Research Institute.

In the following selection, Woods discusses the lives of Lawrence and Lee. The playwrights are best known for their plays Inherit the Wind *and* The Night Thoreau Spent in Jail, *which had sold more than 3 million copies combined by the end of the 1990s. Both these plays, as well as other plays by Lawrence and Lee, question conformity and attempts to limit freedom of thought. Lee's 1994 death ended the writing team's half century of collaboration, which resulted in a seemingly countless number of works in radio, television, cinema, and theater.*

Jerome Lawrence and Robert E. Lee are best known for two plays. *Inherit the Wind* (performed in 1955) and *The Night Thoreau Spent in Jail* (1970), which together had more than three million copies in print by the end of the 1990s. Although their writing partnership, spanning more than a half century, produced significant work in radio, television, and cinema, the stage plays and musicals of Lawrence and Lee seem likely to remain most enduring. *Inherit the Wind* and *The Night Thoreau Spent in Jail*, along with Lawrence and Lee's comedy *Auntie Mame* (1956) and its musical version, *Mame* (1966), have remained in constant production worldwide since first appearing on North American stages. Both *Inherit the Wind* and *The Night Thoreau Spent in Jail* signaled new modes of production in the American commercial theater.

Early Writing Careers

Born three years apart, the two playwrights did not make contact until they were in their mid twenties, although their lives (and careers) were on parallel tracks. Both writers were Ohio natives: Lawrence was born Jerome Lawrence Schwartz on 14 July 1915 in Cleveland, the son of Samuel Schwartz and Sarah (Rogen) Schwartz, while Robert Edwin Lee, born on 15 October 1918, was a native of Elyria, a Cleveland suburb, and the son of C. Melvin and Elvira Taft Lee. Both attended Ohio universities. Lawrence earned a B.A. [bachelor of arts degree] from Ohio State University in Columbus in 1937, and Lee attended Ohio Wesleyan University in Delaware, just north of Columbus, from 1935 to 1937. Both began their professional careers as writers and directors in commercial radio and worked for KMPC in Beverly Hills, California, although at different times. Still, their paths did not cross until January 1942 in New York when, at the instigation of friends, they met and immediately formed a writing partnership. Their first collaboration was "Inside a Kid's Head," produced for the radio program *Columbia Workshop* (and later widely anthologized). By the spring of 1942 the two writers were successful enough that they established an office in Los Angeles, Lee having completed assignments as a writer/director for the Young and Rubicam advertising agency while Lawrence finished his work on the CBS series *They Live Forever*.

Both men went into the armed forces in the summer of 1942, spending most of the World War II years creating and producing programs for the Armed Forces Radio Service. With the war over, both returned to civilian life and continued their partnership as radio writers and directors, creating scripts for such programs as *Favorite Story* (starring Ronald Colman), *The Frank Sinatra Show*, and *Hallmark Playhouse*. In 1948 Lee married Janet Waldo, a radio actress then best known for playing the title role in the popular comedy series *Meet Corliss Archer*. They had two children, Jonathan and Lucy Lee. Lawrence and Lee also landed a contract for their first Broadway show, writing the book for Hugh Martin's musical *Look, Ma, I'm Dancin'!* (1948), a vehicle for comedienne Nancy Walker, choreographed by Jerome Robbins and directed by George S. Abbott. Despite the involvement of three theatrical legends—Walker and Robbins at the beginnings of their careers, Abbott already famous—the musical had only a modest success with 188 performances.

From 1948 through 1954 Lawrence and Lee maintained their focus on radio. As producers, directors, and writers, they were responsible for 299 broadcasts of the weekly series *The Railroad Hour*, while continuing work on *The Halls of Ivy, Favorite Story* (later a television series, 1952–1953), and many other radio and television programs. . . .

A Successful Theater Debut

Lawrence and Lee turned to the stage in the early 1950s, as the advent of commercial network television caused the comedy and serial programming of commercial radio to disappear; radio was beginning its transformation to music and news formats. Their first produced play, which proved to be their greatest success (806 performances), was *Inherit the Wind*. With it they established several patterns that recurred in much of their later work. *Inherit the Wind* is based on an historical event: the Scopes trial of 1925, the prosecution of a Tennessee high-school biology teacher for teaching the theory of evolution. Lawrence and Lee's play fictionalizes the events, however. They wrote in their foreword to the published edition of the text that while the characters of the play are modeled on the figures from that trial, "they have life and language of their

The Scopes *trial of 1925, with attorney Clarence Darrow (left) and prosecutor William Jennings Bryan (right), provided an historical basis for Jerome Lawrence and Robert Edwin Lee's play* Inherit the Wind. *Hilton Archive/Getty Images.*

own—and, therefore, names of their own. . . . *Inherit the Wind* does not pretend to be journalism. It is theatre."

Lawrence and Lee added several characters to the historic record, conflated several more, and sharply condensed the action. In searching for a way to dramatize the religious fundamentalism opposed to the teaching of Darwinism [named for Charles Darwin's theory of evolution], the playwrights invented the character of Reverend Brown and created the revival meeting that opens act 2 to demonstrate vividly the fervor of the townspeople.

By far their most arresting invention, however, was the courtroom confrontation between Henry Drummond—the teacher's defense attorney, loosely based on Clarence Darrow—and Matthew Harrison Brady, the prosecutor derived from William Jennings Bryan. The climax of the play, with Brady on the witness stand as an expert on the Bible, and

Drummond examining him, succinctly and effectively contrasts scientific progress with rigidly literal religiosity. Rationality wins out over irrationality, with Brady ineffectually thumping the witness-stand rail as the curtain falls. Although the historic Darrow did cross-examine the historic Bryan, he did so as part of a team of defense attorneys; virtually all of the dialogue in the play is invented.

While this dramatic climax occurs structurally in the second scene of the second act, the intellectual centerpiece of the play is Drummond's speech in the first scene of the third act, as he waits for the jury's decision. Remembering a flashy rocking horse he coveted as a child, but which proved rotten under the spangles and paint, Drummond articulates his motivating force: "whenever you see something bright, shining, perfect-seeming ... look behind the paint! And if it's a lie—show it up for what it really is!" This message is reiterated in the final scene by Rachel Brown, the Reverend Brown's daughter, who has finally learned to welcome all ideas, not repressing those that challenge and thus create discomfort. Both Drummond's rocking-horse speech and Rachel's discovery help to widen the underlying themes of the play.

A Focus on Freedom of Thought

For Lawrence and Lee, it was clear that evolution and Darwinism represented progress and the growth of the human spirit, in opposition to the repressive censorship of Brady and Reverend Brown and their efforts to block rational development. The conflict of the play is not between evolution and creationism (a term not in common usage when it was written), therefore, but between freedom of thought and repression of free inquiry. By giving the play that focus, and also by avoiding close reproduction of the historic events in Tennessee, the playwrights were able to emphasize the broader and more-universal aspects of the conflict. The invented figure of Rachel Brown, who at first glance might be mistaken for the schoolteacher's stereotypical romantic interest, becomes— from this perspective—the fulcrum of the play. Rachel's journey from unthinking acceptance of her father's literal interpretation of Genesis to understanding that she bears the responsibility for developing her own opinions is the voyage to self-consciousness that is only possible with freedom of thought.

Inherit the Wind has been translated into more than thirty languages and appeared once as a major Hollywood movie (1960) and in three television adaptations (1965, 1988, 1999), in addition to constant stage production. Its enduring appeal certainly stems, at least in part, from its focus on themes suggested by the Scopes trial rather than on a re-creation of the trial itself as an historical docudrama.

Lawrence and Lee intended *Inherit the Wind* as a comment on Senator Joseph McCarthy's campaigns against communism, which the playwrights regarded as a thinly veiled attack on the freedoms of speech and thought. Many of their later plays also use historical events and characters as springboards to explore contemporary issues, often fictionalizing real people and their actions in order to avoid the limitations of documentary.

Effective Drama

The playwrights' first major success also shares with virtually all of the later work a sharp awareness of dramatic effectiveness: finding visual images, patterns of movement and sound, or other essentially nonliterary means of conveying meaning. The closing moment of *Inherit the Wind*, as Drummond weighs and then claps together the Bible and Charles Darwin's *On the Origin of Species* (1859), is one such image. Another, more extended [moment], comes in the revival meeting that opens the second act, with its rising emotional frenzy. Similar theatrical images exist throughout the playwrights' work.

Inherit the Wind also signaled the growing importance of professional regional theaters distant from the commercial theater center of New York City. First produced at Margo Jones's pioneering theater in Dallas, Theatre '55 (the name changed with the year), and only then given a commercial production, *Inherit the Wind* was among the first major American plays to be produced regionally before, rather than after, its Broadway premiere. The standard production process, as it existed in the early 1950s, was to have plays produced directly for the New York stage, with out-of-town tryouts for four to six weeks prior to the New York opening. Frantic rewrites were the norm out of town, and it was not uncommon for the writer's original concept and tone to vanish completely in the effort to make a piece commercially viable. Plays that failed in their initial New York productions generally disappeared without a trace; lacking the distinction conferred by success in New York, they rarely were produced by theaters (whether professional or amateur) elsewhere.

Lawrence and Lee consistently sought alternatives to that commercial production process, having experienced the less frantic and more effective tryout pattern with *Inherit the Wind*. This intent led to their creation of the American Playwrights Theatre (APT) in 1965. The APT sought unproduced plays from established playwrights, then distributed plays approved by an evaluative committee to member theaters. If enough theaters optioned APT selections for production, the organization guaranteed exclusive performance rights for a period of two years. At its height, the APT included more than 160 theaters as members, ranging from professional regional theaters to academic and amateur community organizations.

Leaders in Alternative Theater

The signal APT success was Lawrence and Lee's own *The Night Thoreau Spent in Jail*, produced entirely outside commercial venues. With 155 productions under APT auspices from 1970

23

through 1973, *The Night Thoreau Spent in Jail* has never been produced in New York; yet it, along with *Inherit the Wind*, remains in the worldwide repertory.

The Night Thoreau Spent in Jail dramatizes the historical incident in which Henry David Thoreau, protesting the Mexican-American War of 1846–1848, went to jail for refusing to pay his taxes. Lawrence and Lee's text utilizes a fluid structure, with characters and events swirling in expressionistic patterns around the central figure of Thoreau, in jail throughout the play. Each of the flashback scenes, and those set in the jail itself, reveal aspects of Thoreau's character and philosophy, constructing, by the end of the play, a composite portrait explaining his actions. The structure of the play is reminiscent of the epic drama championed by Bertolt Brecht: short scenes connected thematically rather than by the logical causality of the well-made play of realism. The opening exchange of dialogue between Ralph Waldo Emerson and his wife, Lydian, about their confusion over Thoreau's given name sounds the theme of Thoreau's self-creation, reinforced immediately by Thoreau's renaming of himself and his rejection of conformity. . . .

While its structure reflects the kind of theatrical experimentation particularly prominent in the latter half of the 1960s, *The Night Thoreau Spent in Jail* also comments as clearly on contemporary social and political events as did *Inherit the Wind*. Thoreau's rejection of his government's involvement in the Mexican-American War mirrors in direct ways the public's growing rejection of the U.S. military involvement in South Vietnam; indeed, the first production of the play in 1970 was abruptly closed when campuses across the country erupted after shootings [of students by National Guardsmen] at Kent State University in Ohio during war protests. The continuous-production history of the play suggests, however, that it is no more tied to the immediate issues that inspired it than was *Inherit the Wind*. . . .

International Success

A similar challenge to conventional authority is the mainspring of Lawrence and Lee's third enduring success, *Auntie Mame* (1956), adapted from the 1955 best-selling comic novel by Patrick Dennis. Opening in New York while *Inherit the Wind* continued its initial run, *Auntie Mame* ran for 639 performances in New York and had a similar international success. Lawrence and Lee's script was transferred with only minor changes to the screen in 1958 (with Rosalind Russell, the original star). The partners further adapted their script with a score by Jerry Herman for the smash hit musical version, *Mame*, in 1966; it ran for 1,508 performances and was filmed in 1974 from a screenplay by Paul Zindel (with Lucille Ball in the title role). Both the play and the musical are frequently produced.

Patrick Dennis's novel of the adventures of a madcap free spirit and the nephew she inherits became, in Lawrence and Lee's hands, an episodic comedy with serious undertones. The Depression of the 1930s figures largely in the comedy, as do satiric thrusts at ethnic prejudices, trendy education, hidebound conformism, pretentious intellectualism, and social snobbery. The constant redecoration of Mame's Beekman Place apartment in New York provides its own running satire of fashion, and the guests present at the cocktail party in the first scene of the play are a satiric portrait of fashionable society.

Auntie Mame is more than clever satire, however, as well as being more than a star vehicle for the performer cast in the title role, although some reviewers initially dismissed the piece as being one or the other. (The episodic structure of the comedy also misled a few reviewers, who criticized it as a musical without songs.) The play celebrates freedom of thought (and speech), particularly in Mame's defiance of the anti-Semitism of the Upsons in act 2, and also emphasizes individualism. That it does so comically rather than in a serious dramatic context may have obscured the degree to which *Auntie Mame* shares concerns with *Inherit the Wind* and *The Night Thoreau Spent in Jail.* The episodic structure, treated as a weakness by reviewers of the first production, in fact permitted the playwrights to convey important plot elements through action rather than the narrative of the novel. . . .

Unlike *Inherit the Wind* and *The Night Thoreau Spent in Jail, Auntie Mame* is not based on an historical event (however fictionalized), nor does it comment on contemporaneous controversies. Its presentation of the dangers of conformity, however, does reflect a concern of the mid 1950s. . . . Lawrence and Lee's comedy shares the concerns for individualism and freedom of ideas present in their two more-serious plays.

Having been based on a popular novel, *Auntie Mame* also was typical of another aspect of Lawrence and Lee's work: the commissioned adaptation. As radio writers, Lawrence and Lee had adapted hundreds of works of fiction for *Favorite Story* and had also done a long series of musical adaptations for *The Railroad Hour* from 1948 through 1954. As theater writers they continued the practice, frequently alternating original works with adaptations. Thus, their book for *Shangri-La* (1956), the musical version of James Hilton's novel *Lost Horizon* (1933), followed *Inherit the Wind* (and was closely followed by *Auntie Mame*). Their original play *The Gang's All Here* (1959) opened shortly before their 1959 adaptation of Harry Golden's *Only in America* (1958).

Fictionalized History

Many of the plays employ Lawrence and Lee's fascination with historic incidents and figures, usually fictionalized to greater or lesser degrees. *The Gang's All Here* uses many of the character traits of President Warren G. Harding for its President Griffith P. Hastings. The play is set in the early 1920s and embroils President Hastings in a series of scandals that suggest the Teapot Dome [a scandal involving bribes accepted by

Harding's secretary of the interior]. By making Hastings fictional, the playwrights are again free from the need to be entirely faithful to fact and so can suggest that Hastings, learning finally the depth of the corruption he has permitted to blossom, commits suicide at the conclusion of the play. The cheerful corruption of President Hastings's aides is more obvious—and hence less ominous—than the corruption American audiences have discovered in presidential politics since the play was first produced, at the end of the [Dwight D.] Eisenhower presidency. . . .

Several of the Lawrence and Lee plays show an individual corrupted by the larger society. In *The Gang's All Here* a jovially mediocre senator becomes a dangerously mediocre president, led into corruption by the mendacity of his rapacious advisers and confidants, while in *Diamond Orchid* a thoroughly amoral young woman sleeps her way to power and enormous riches as her lover/husband becomes a military dictator in a South American country, only to discover the emptiness of her soul when faced with incurable cancer. In the playwrights' final play, *Whisper in the Mind* (1990), the historic figure of Anton Mesmer misinterprets his abilities to treat patients, bringing his passionate belief in the power of the mind in conflict with rational science, made concrete by the figure of Benjamin Franklin.

Mesmer was in fact investigated in late-eighteenth-century Paris by a commission chaired by Franklin, then the U.S. ambassador to France. Lawrence and Lee were brought to the story by writer Norman Cousins, who had explored the idea of the ability of the mind to transform pain in his best-selling *Anatomy of an Illness as Perceived by the Patient: Reflection on Healing and Regeneration* (1979). As the historic incident was obscure, and the figure of Mesmer little known to the general public, the playwrights felt secure in expanding the facts, linking Mesmer and Franklin through the ailing daughter of one of Franklin's Parisian romances and locating the young girl's mental instability in the context of the instabilities of France itself a few years prior to the French Revolution.

The conflict between observable phenomena and the non-observable workings of the mind was a logical choice for the playwrights, particularly when the conflict could be personalized in two major figures of individualism: Mesmer, regarded historically as a charlatan, and Franklin, a symbol of the rights of the individual, placed in the position of evaluating those rights against the demands of the larger society. In many ways *Whisper in the Mind* was a fitting final work for the playwrights, bringing together the concerns explored over a half century of writing as partners; their first produced work, "Inside a Kid's Head," had explored how the mind worked (albeit comically), while their last play examined efforts to understand, and harness, the mind's power.

A Half-Century Partnership Ends

In many respects Lawrence and Lee were among the last of the professional commercial playwrights in the United States, a tradition continued only by their younger contemporary, Neil Simon. Lawrence and Lee were constant presences in the commercial New York stage, from their dramatic debut in 1955 with *Inherit the Wind* through the production of *First Monday in October* a little more than two decades later. During those twenty-three years, they were represented by eleven plays in New York, along with three premiered elsewhere. Although it may seem contradictory to hail them as commercial playwrights, given their efforts (through the American Playwrights Theatre and other ventures) to undercut the New York dominance of the American stage, Lawrence and Lee regularly wrote for the commercial stage. They accepted commissions and created adaptations and musicalizations; in short, they were professional writers. Although their stage careers could not match the sheer volume of their work for commercial radio, their theatrical dramas, comedies, and musicals share a common sensibility: the responsibility and privilege of the individual to develop and promulgate ideas, freely and without restraint, whether from a government or from a dominant social order. That ideal animates most of the plays, in varying ways. The works Lawrence and Lee adapted and the plays that originated with them are remarkably consistent.

Lee's death in 1994 brought the partnership to a close. Although both Lee and Lawrence produced dramas, nonfiction, and fiction individually, their most enduring work was created as partners. Lee died shortly after the revised version of *Whisper in the Mind* ended its premiere run at the Missouri Repertory Theatre in Kansas City; whether this last play will have a future life is not yet clear. It is certain, however, that with *Inherit the Wind, Auntie Mame*, and *The Night Thoreau Spent in Jail*, Jerome Lawrence and Robert E. Lee crafted major contributions to the world dramatic repertory while creating a body of significant work that is frequently challenging and always dealing with important social, political, and ethical issues.

Lawrence and Lee Talk About Playwriting

Jerome Lawrence and Robert E. Lee, Interviewed by Christopher Meeks

Christopher Meeks teaches English at Santa Monica College and creative writing at various other California colleges. He is also a writer of fiction and plays.

In the following article, Meeks interviews the playwrights of In-herit the Wind, Jerome Lawrence and Robert Edwin Lee. In the interview, Lawrence and Lee debate why playwriting is the great-est sport in the world. Included are tips for new playwrights and reasons why the writing duo believes young playwrights have an advantage over experienced ones. They also discuss the impor-tance of having a creative memory, why comedies need to be se-rious and why drama needs humor, and a playwright's cultural responsibility.

About as far from Broadway as the US land mass permits live two of the more active playwrights the New York stages serve up: Jerome Lawrence and Robert E. Lee. For more than 43 years [as of 1986], they have been looking behind the [outward appearance] of America and showing it for what it is. From the hilarious *Auntie Mame* and its musical version, *Mame*, to the provoking *The Night Thoreau Spent in Jail*, the two writers have always punctured pomposity. They have writ-ten 20 major plays, including the classic *Inherit the Wind*. . . .

Success of the Beginning Writer

[Christopher Meeks for] *Writer's Digest* [WD]: You once said, Bob, that you enjoyed teaching new playwrights, particularly undergraduates. Why?

Christopher Meeks, "The Greatest Sport in the World," *Writer's Digest*, vol. 66, March 1986. Reproduced by permission of the author.

[*Robert E. "Bob"] Lee*: I think there's a marvelous plasticity to people who are approaching writing seriously for the first time. You hear them say: "Wow! You can do this, you can do that, you can play God. You can create these characters and make them do what you want them to do."

WD: Take them to the sun and back.

Lee: And faster. The imagination is C-squared—swifter than the speed of light.

WD: Kurt Vonnegut once said he believes he's successful because he hasn't "mastered" writing yet, that he always approaches it as a beginner. It sounds like that's what you're saying.

[*Jerome "Jerry"] Lawrence*: Every play that Bob and I start to write together—or separately, which we do sometimes—we feel is really our first play and that we're starting from the beginning.

One reason that approach is good for all writers is that the so-called experienced writers don't take chances. They keep harking back to their wounds. And they say, "I did that, it was a flop, it didn't work." And that limits you.

I think Bob and I still consider ourselves young playwrights. A cop stopped me once for making a wrong turn, and he said, "Have you ever been arrested?" and I said, "Only emotionally." He didn't understand that at all. I think I froze at 18. I just feel everything we write, every script we write, we're handing in as beginning writers.

Lee: A sudden success can paralyze a beginning writer; he may spend the rest of his life trying to figure out what he did right.

Lawrence: [Playwrights] Moss Hart and Bob Anderson went to see *The Seven Year Itch*, which was an experimental comedy—breaking all rules—by George Axelrod, who in his next play called a playwright a "playwrote," and then became a playwrote himself because *The Seven Year Itch* was so successful that he never returned to the theatre, he never took a chance again after his second play flopped. At *The Seven Year Itch*, Moss Hart turned to Bob Anderson and said, "They'd kill us if we wrote this play." But it was a first play by a young playwright, and the critics raved about it.

Lee: You see, a younger playwright is a "terra incognita"—a new creative landfall to be sighted. On the other hand, a known playwright wears the albatross of his own reputation around his neck. He is a *target*.

I've got to tell you a curious thing about life—and it's an observation about the flexibility of memory. My recollection is that [playwright and director] Garson Kanin made the remark that Jerry just mentioned to *you*, Jerry, after you both had seen David Mamet's *A Life in the Theatre*. Gar commented: "The critics would have fractured us if we'd written that play." I remember something one way, Jerry recalls it another. Neither of us is lying. It is simply the parallax of personalities. The greatest miracle of memory isn't its infallibility, but its malleability.

Creative Memory

Lawrence: Every playwright must have *creative* memory. You take your past and personal history, and stick to it literally, but there's no such thing as literal history. You have the obligation to be creative with personal memory and with history. Facts change depending on which part of the elephant you touch.[1]

Lee: Now that's not dishonest. For example, when we wrote *Inherit the Wind*, people asked why we changed the names. One of the reasons is we wanted the freedom that Jerry speaks of. When we did *The Night Thoreau Spent in Jail*, we were dealing with [writers Henry David] Thoreau, [Ralph Waldo] Emerson. We were dealing with people who were absolute,

1. The reference is to a parable of perception in which three blind men each describe an elephant, which they cannot see, completely differently because they are touching different parts of it.

and we could not have that freedom. Whenever you're dealing with historically based material, just remember: [Ancient Greek historian] Herodotus didn't have a tape recorder. No one knows *precisely* what was said (or not said). The dramatist must be granted freedom of invention.

Lawrence: Verisimilitude can be more truthful than truth. Verisimilitude, according to the dictionary, is the *appearance* of truth. But sometimes you want a higher truth; by boiling something down to the essence of it, you may get a higher truth and know that the essence is completely fictional. It can somehow be less of a lie than something that factually happened.

The major scene in our play is Thoreau's big showdown with Emerson. Well, there's no historical record that the meeting ever happened. But the greatest authority on Thoreau, Walter Harding, who is head of the Thoreau Society and has written his best biography, came to see the show and told us, "I finally really understand the relationship between Emerson and Thoreau." Yet, it's something we entirely created out of what might have happened or could have happened or *should* have happened.

Lee: It was our task, as playwrights, to extrapolate what was said.

One other thing about memory—about the changing of memory—that's also very important: You forget things. You have to have *selective* memory. And there are certain things that simply do not need to be carried around. . . .

Comedy and Collaboration

WD: You once said, Jerry, that a certain play wasn't "serious enough to be a comedy." How does humor enter into your own works?

Lawrence: We always say that all our serious plays are funny and all our funny plays are serious. It's more important that a comedy have something really basic to say because then you can take off and be funny about it. There are, alas, so many young playwrights who take themselves so seriously that they are afraid of humor. Wit might trivialize their profound work.

The best playwrights—Tennessee Williams, for instance—will puncture the most serious moment with an outrageous laugh. The audience delights in it. They need the relief. They need laughter—or what [journalist] Norman Cousins calls "inner jogging"—for the joy of life. The more an audience laughs, the more it feels. [William] Shakespeare knew this—there's comedy in his most serious plays.

WD: What concerns you when you write? Is there a particular attitude you're aware of?

Lee: That you're in a partnership with your reader—and your audience, your listener, your viewer. This is one of the reasons I can't understand why there are not more partnerships among writers. I must have taught more than a hundred students in graduate classes, and I have never succeeded in bringing two of them together. There's a fierce—and often self-destructive—independence about playwrights. They want to swim the Atlantic alone. The resistance to partnership is very strong. Both Jerry and I are very blessed that we are able to flourish as a team. The reasons are partly that we're very different. Jerry's viewpoint is often considerably at odds with mine, but who wants a partner who just says yes to everything?

Lawrence: If he said yes to me all the time, I wouldn't give him 50% of my money. [Laughs.] That's an old joke.

WD: How do you work together? What's a day with Lawrence and Lee like?

Lawrence: It depends on what we're working on. We try to work six days a week and, if we're lucky, get five pages down every day. When we're actively working on a play, we usually are face to face. Sometimes, when there's heavy traffic, we're on an open phone line. We dialogue together and we talk out plots and characters together. We try to be face to face as often as possible.

Lee: On prose, books, short stories, articles, we write individually. And sometimes, when we have to write a piece we both sign, one of us drafts it and the other one punches it up.

If one of us says no to an idea or some dialogue or whatever, he has the obligation to come up with something better. We work "positively." . . .

A Playwright's Cultural Responsibility

WD: Steering in another direction: I think there's a general belief that playwriting is like poetry—fun to tinker at but something that can't bring home the bacon. Obviously you two have made money, but is it a profession to encourage?

Lawrence: It's a difficult profession, so you've got to have a concurrent occupation. You've got to have a money-making job at the same time you're writing plays, and then eventually playwriting will support you.

Lee: *Anything* that's hard to do is difficult to get into. Forgive me, but I think that's a foolish question. It's not analogous to poetry because there is no clear box office for poetry.

We will need plays, always. It is a standard commodity. The worse the times are, the more people will need to be relieved of reality. During the Depression, the theatre flourished. Not financially so much as artistically.

Lawrence: Also during the war. Then, as [playwrights] Howard Lindsay and Russel Crouse used to tell us, Times Square was blacked out. There were no lights in the city.

Lee: The news all over the world was terrible.

Lawrence: Terrible. And [Lindsay and Crouse] said at the end of *Life With Father*, which was about the Gilded Age (there was the red plush and the family and the certainties of the 1910s), nobody left the theater. After the curtain fell, they just sat. They let that glow warm them before going out into the dark night.

The theatre means many things to many people. To be a playwright, I think you've got to feel the pulse of your times and be a little bit of a prophet. And your play has got to be *about* something. If someone says, "What's your play about?" and all you can answer is, "It's about two and a half hours long," then the only answer back is, "It's two and a half hours too long." It has to have a spine, it has to have some meaning, it has to offer some illumination.

Good Plays Are Possessed by Ideas

Lee: It's got to have more than a spine. It's got to have a motor.

Lawrence: Every *scene* has to have a motor in it. That's the best test. If a scene has drive, it goes somewhere.

WD: Both a spine and a motor?

Lee: It's a mixed metaphor—excuse us. A motor with a spine, or a spine with a motor is bad imagery.

WD: Is the spine "theme"?

Lee: The word *theme* is not a helpful word for a practical writer. Let the critics or the audience talk about the theme. You write the play because you are possessed. You're possessed by an idea, by a passion. You see, theme has a surgical feel to it.

Lawrence: *Theme* sounds like *thesis*—it's an academic word. Your play has got to have some solid structure, some *spine*. You couldn't walk around very well if you didn't have a spine. A play's a human being.

When Bob said each scene has a motor, it means you don't start and finish each scene in the same place. It has to have some thrust, some drive. It has to go someplace. It can't stand still. Stasis is dullness in the theatre.

Now we go beyond that to a spine, which means every scene in a play, and every play itself, must stand up. I think *spine* is a very good word.

Lee: *Spine* and *theme* are fancy Christmas-ball words. There's got to be that purring, driving brrrrrrrrrrrrr.

Lawrence: The breath of life.

Lee: Yes! The élan [creative spark] that makes a play. Without it, we couldn't write *Simulation*, a TV movie we just finished about ten students at Stanford University who are studying arms control. Up at Stanford, they insisted, "Come up here; you've got to see these students at work." All of a sudden we were *thrust* into the midst of their situation, and we realized we could hear the motor running.

Lawrence: There was passion there, there was commitment there, there was reason for their going to that class every day. We could hear every one of their motors running, which meant their brains were running, their hearts were ticking, their blood was flowing through their veins. You know, that's what we're trying to say in perhaps many wild, unrelated metaphors.

WD: How do you find a motor?

Lee: The people. The people in the play rev it up. What happens when Jerry and I are writing is all of a sudden the people begin to move, they begin to demand things.

Lawrence: Let the reins a little loose and let your horse go up different roads.

Lee: That's an old Emerson point. He says, "When a man is lost in the woods on horseback, what he should do is let the reins fall loose and let the horse go home."

Lawrence: Robert Frost has a poem called "The Road Not Taken." Let yourself go down untrodden paths. It's terribly important. And if you *really* understand your characters—what Bob started to say more eloquently than I—they will help you write your play. . . .

Tapping into Anger

WD: I've been in classes, seen people in classes who are eager to write, and they have talent, but they don't know what to write about. How do you get them to find a purpose?

Lee: Ask one question.

WD: What's that?

Lee: What makes you mad?

WD: What makes you mad?

Lee: What do you really care about?

Lawrence: What gives you goose-bumps?

Lee: What bugs you?

Lawrence: Reveal something. Dig out something about yourself that you haven't even revealed to yourself. Dig out something in history. Dig out something in your parents, in your government, in your church, in your friends, but especially in yourself.

Lee: Write with a spade. Go back to *Inherit the Wind*. We were bugged by the McCarthy era. We tried to write *Inherit the Wind* as a parable to show the disastrous things that can happen if you try to legislate thought.

Lawrence: Thought control.

Lee: We were bugged by the Vietnam war, so we wrote *The Night Thoreau Spent in Jail*.

Lawrence: We were bugged by censorship. *First Monday in October* is not about the Supreme Court as much as it is about a battle against censorship and a battle against the control of all our lives by the multinationals, by this cabal of unseen men who can suppress inventions, who can do all sorts of things that can diminish our lives.

Lee: This bugs me. And if nothing bugs you, I don't think you should write.

Lawrence: It's very difficult. It's difficult because revelation is the subtext of a script and the subtext of a life and very difficult to get onto paper.

The Greatest Sport in the World

Lawrence: Keep writing, write every day, keep at it, keep going, keep doing some new works, new plays of size and meaning.

Lee: With motors.

Lawrence: Motors in every scene.

WD: What about subplots?

Lee: Don't think about plots. There is *no* such thing as a plot. There is only what interesting people do.

Lawrence: People are interested in people. The human animal.

Lee: You don't have to think in terms of a plot. Think of what do these people do. Then all of a sudden they will weave their own plot.

WD: I see formulas where you set up a couple groups and they sort of interweave.

Lee: Strike the word *formula*. Never use the word *formula*. There is no "tao," no pattern, no modus from a "master." [Spanish poet] Antonio Machado speaks eloquently of a traveler walking across a meadow, he is following no path, for there is no path to follow. And when he looks back, all he sees is the crushed grass where his own steps have fallen.

Lawrence: It's a patrol where you are your own "point man." The playwright is in a position of great danger. There is fear and beauty on what [actress] Stella Adler calls "the platform." Glory and disaster—mixed, inseparable, unpredictable.

Lee: Think how impossible it is, Chris: We're doomed. We are absolutely doomed on this planet. You, Jerry, myself. A few months, a few years, and where'll we be? Yet we are pervaded by this totally irrational optimism!

Lawrence: We wake up every morning. We get out of bed.

Lee: Better than that—we *dare* to wake up every morning, *dare* to get out of bed! We *dare* to put things on the stage. We *care* to play God as playwrights. It's the greatest sport in the world.

Lawrence and Lee Promote the Dignity of Every Individual Mind

Nena Couch

Nena Couch is curator of the Jerome Lawrence and Robert E. Lee Theatre Research Institute at the Ohio State University and a professor in the university's Department of Theatre.

In the following article, Nena Couch interviews the playwrights of Inherit the Wind, *Jerome Lawrence and Robert Edwin Lee. According to Couch, Lawrence and Lee's attempts to "rough up the consciousness" account for their ability to effectively reach audiences with their plays' messages. The playwrights explain how freedom of thought and the power of the individual are the leading ideas of their plays. And these ideas not only make their plays interesting, say the playwrights, but also influence audiences to apply these values in the real world. Lawrence and Lee embody these ideas, in part, by looking forward—not back on their past success.*

As one of the great partnerships in theatre, Jerome Lawrence and Robert E. Lee have written some of the longest running and most widely produced plays of [the twentieth] century, many of which have been called contemporary theatre classics. But their proudest accolade is when they are described as "The Thinking-Person's Playwrights." Ironically, since they most often work as a team, Lawrence and Lee have been dedicated, enthusiastic proponents of the individual. This commitment to the "dignity of the individual human mind," apparent in their first Broadway success, *Look, Ma, I'm*

Nena Couch, "An Interview with Jerome Lawrence and Robert E. Lee," *Studies in American Drama, 1945–Present*, vol. 7, 1992, pp. 3–5, 7–18. Copyright © 1992 by The Ohio State University. All rights reserved. Reproduced by permission.

Dancin'! in 1948, has continued to their newest play, *Whisper in the Mind* which premiered on October 5, 1990 [and became the final play Lawrence and Lee produced together]. Be that individual a delightful and free-thinking Mame (*Auntie Mame* and *Mame*) who urges us to discover new things about ourselves and the world, a Drummond (*Inherit the Wind*) whose balancing of the Bible and [the theory of evolution introduced by Charles] Darwin shows us that the open and inquiring mind is our champion against censorship, a Countess Aurelia (*Dear World*) who proves to us that "one person can change the world," a Supreme Court Justice Dan Snow (*First Monday in October*) who fights for the light for everyone, or a Thoreau (*The Night Thoreau Spent in Jail*) who is not afraid to march to a different drummer, Lawrence and Lee have populated stages all over the world with sometimes serious, sometimes witty, but always passionately committed, individuals. The playwrights are, as they say of Mame, enemies of "anything which places corsets on our minds or our soaring spirits." As [nineteenth-century American writer] Henry David Thoreau says for them, "Nobody leaves us with a smooth surface. We rough up the consciousness, scrape the moss off young minds." . . .

This interview was conducted via telephone conference call on January 24, 1991. Lawrence and Lee discussed their work in the context of the theme of an exhibit, "'Roughing Up the Consciousness': the Plays of Jerome Lawrence and Robert E. Lee," mounted by the interviewer [Nena Couch] in the Philip Sills Exhibit Hall, The Ohio State University [OSU] Libraries, September–November 1990. . . .

Early Influences

Couch: I see "roughing up the consciousness" in all your plays in one way or another. What interests me particularly is what in your early lives shaped you individually and then what brought you together.

Do your friends a favour—give them the coupon overleaf so they can enjoy the show too.

Beatrice Lillie

as

"Auntie Mame"

with
Florence DESMOND

ADELPHI
THEATRE · STRAND W.C.2 TEM 7611

MON.-FRI. at 7.30.   SATS. 5.30 & 8.30.   MATINEE WED. 2.30
Stalls 20/- 15/6 10/6.   Dress Circle 17/6 12/6 8/6   Upper Circle 6/-

A London theater advertisement promoting the Adelphi Theatre's adaptation of Jerome Lawrence and Robert Edwin Lee's humorous play Auntie Mame. © Amoret Tanner/ Alamy.

Lee: Well, originally I didn't intend to make writing my career. I was determined to be an astronomer, so I went to Ohio

Wesleyan which operated the giant telescope at Perkins Observatory in concert with OSU. Then I got interested in communications. And I began to get the feeling that somehow communicating with the stars and planets was pretty much a one-way street. So I plunged into broadcasting which led to my meeting Jerry in New York and getting to work with him. Ironically, we had never met in Ohio, though we were both Buckeyes [Ohioans], born and schooled thirty miles apart.

Lawrence: I always wanted to be a writer. My father was a printer, my mother was an unpublished poet. The only deviation I had from playwriting was as a small-town newspaperman, which supplied me with masses of material for the writing years that followed.

Lee: All of our early radio writing, individually, then happily as a team, taught us to write for the ear. . . .

Lawrence: The exhibit you mounted, Nena, was appropriately titled "Roughing Up the Consciousness" because that's what both of us have tried to do as writers from the very start.

Lee: I subscribe to that because I know as an aborning [beginning] scientist that nothing really adheres to a smooth surface. If you're aiming an idea at another mind, you hope it's not so slick it won't stick. You've got to ruffle up the smoothness of that recipient consciousness, otherwise your ideas will just slide off, slip away.

Lawrence: By "roughing up" we don't mean "beating up" (we're violently opposed to violence), but "shaking up" our audiences and, even more importantly, ourselves. We've also called that "sandpapering the soul," a kind of abrasivenes which digs beneath the false surface, the gilt (or guilt) surface and probes down there where the truth might be found. . . .

Prequel to *Inherit the Wind*

Lee: I think there is too much lubrication in life. I'd much rather see sparks than grease.

Lawrence: That's why we called one of our plays *Sparks Fly Upward*. Now here we have *The Angels Weep*. Reading it in this issue might make you think the second half of this bi-play is a sequel to *Inherit the Wind*. Actually, it's a *prequel*, much like what [author] Lillian Hellman did a few years after *The Little Foxes* by writing *Another Part of the Forest*, which is about the same characters, Regina and Birdie and Oscar, many years earlier.

Lee: The lawyer-on-trial in *The Angels Weep* is Henry Drummond earlier in his career. His speech in *Inherit the Wind*, chronologically many years later, explains how he felt when he himself was unjustly accused of being a near-criminal:

> It's the loneliest feeling in the world—to find yourself standing up when everybody else is sitting down. . . . I know. I know what it feels like. Walking down an empty street listening to the sound of your own footsteps. Shutters closed, blinds drawn, doors locked against you. And you aren't sure whether you're walking toward something—or just walking away.

Lawrence: Both halves of *The Angels Weep* take place in the same courtroom in the same city, Los Angeles, the City of Angels. The first half is a "Sanity Hearing" concerning a woman who adored her father who had owned a department store; now her sanity is being questioned because she refuses to sell the store. This is vaguely related to a play we wrote early on called *Eclipse*, about my maternal grandfather who owned a family department store in Ohio. We never went beyond a first draft of it. I guess we didn't have the professional know-how or the guts in those days to rewrite and polish and perfect, which we've learned to do since.

Lee: Hopefully. You know, a lot of promising projects get sideswiped in the traffic of activity. I think every creative career leaves some abandoned vehicles along the side of the road.

Couch: Do you ever go back afterwards?

Lawrence: Sure. And *The Angels Weep* is a case in point. Though none of the actual material is used here, it is related to two of our previous works.

Lee: But it goes beyond to explore the psyche of lawyers and the court system, adding the Godot-ish [referring to Samuel Beckett's play *Waiting for Godot*, in which two characters wait for someone named Godot] characters of the two cleaning people, who can be played, incidentally, by two men, two women, or one of each, by whites, by blacks, by Hispanics, by any casting you want to use.

Lawrence: As long as they're truthful actors.

Couch: Which makes it flexible for all sorts of groups to produce. . . . Could we go to the radio plays and talk about that experience? Bob used the words "writing for the ear." I consider your radio plays a fascinating part of your work.

Radio vs. Theatre

Lee: Nena, you know that some of our foremost playwrights began by writing radio plays: Arthur Miller, Arthur Laurents, John Patrick . . .

Lawrence: . . . Robert Anderson, Neil Simon.

Lee: In the early days, when we were all making the transition into theatre, none of us wanted to be characterized as just radio writers.

Lawrence: Note that none of the dramatists we mentioned ever listed radio credits in their theatre Playbill bios.

Lee: That's because the New York critics thought that anybody writing for radio had to be a "commercial hack," forgetting the great writers in this medium like Norman Corwin and Archibald MacLeish, who wrote poetry and literature. And who knows? Maybe even we did occasionally.

Lawrence: I remember flying to New York, as national president of the Radio Writers Guild, to appear before the Council of the Authors League. I was appalled when a wonderful playwright like Elmer Rice said scornfully: "We don't want to have anything to do with you soap-opera writers."

Lee: But Elmer, who was a splendidly abrasive man, changed his tune completely.

Lawrence: Later he had a lot to do with the formation of American Playwrights Theatre, and came to know that everybody connected with it began as a radio writer. Live radio provided roots for the living stage. And none of us had ever touched a soap-opera with a ten-foot laundry pole.

Lee: Effective radio drama (and we directed most of our broadcasts) was a tapestry of words, music, sound.

Lawrence: It was theatre of the imagination.

Lee: Perhaps radio drama was much closer to theatre than motion pictures or television turned out to be. The visual media depend on the impact of spectacle. But both radio and theatre depend on *words* to fire the imagination.

Lawrence: Words and ideas made vivid.

Lee: If the quintessence of theatre is [William] Shakespeare, he proved that the ultimate theatrical experience is primarily verbal.

Lawrence: His words create spectacle in the imagination of his audiences and readers. There are no roller skates, no cats[1] in Shakespeare.

Lee: And very few car chases. . . .

Capturing the Idea and the Individual

Couch: Certainly the IDEA (that should be in capital letters!) figures in all your work—Drummond in *Inherit the Wind*: "An idea is a greater monument than a cathedral."

Lawrence: And certainly Auntie Mame who not only opens windows, but minds!

---

1. This appears to be a dig at the popularity on Broadway of composer Andrew Lloyd Webber, whose long-running productions *Starlight Express* and *Cats* featured actors on skates and costumed as cats, respectively.

Couch: And Guzmano, the [humanitarian Albert] Schweitzer-like doctor-philosopher of *Sparks Fly Upward* who worries about the entire Western world "Trading in the human mind for a computing machine."

Lee: My wife is sure the computer is "Big Brother" [the fictional dictator in George Orwell's novel *1984*].

Couch: And there's a wonderful speech that follows: "One!" . . .

Lawrence: . . . "There is no number larger than ONE." And when they ask Senator Orton what he thinks of Guzmano, he says, "It's hard to argue with a good cello." He means that Guzmano makes a symphony of ideas, deep-sounding music out of language and thought.

Lee: I'm glad you brought that up because in many respects *Sparks Fly Upward*, alias *Diamond Orchid*, is one of our favorite plays, partly I suppose because it's a slightly forgotten child and we think it had some of our best work in it.

Lawrence: Almost if not all of our plays share the theme of the dignity of every individual mind, and that mind's life-long battle against limitation and censorship.

Lee: People usually say that *First Monday in October* is about the first woman on the Supreme Court. Of course it is, but mostly it's about the real obscenity—censorship, and it attacks the kind of world-controllers who want to diminish our lives, limit our horizons.

Couch: One of my favorite speeches in *First Monday* is Dan Snow's about the light: "NOBODY has the right to turn on the darkness."

Lawrence: That's it. That's the point of it. You mustn't let yourself be pushed into the empty dark. You've got to keep looking for the light. You've got to keep sandpapering things until the light shines through. It's all related. *The Gang's All Here* is the probing of the presidency, not just *a* president, but *the* presidency. And *Only in America* is tearing the scab off the wounds of bigotry and racism then applying the healing ointment of humor and understanding.

Lee: And *Whisper in the Mind* thinks aloud about the tremendously important point that even a good idea, if it is misconceived, can backfire, can be harmful. If you try to get things too well ordered, your ego shouting that you've got everything figured out, all truths saddled and ready to ride the universal derby, you're in real trouble.

Lawrence: Getting a play on paper is a long-distance marathon. It takes stick-to-it-tiveness to create a play, to refine it, and polish it. You must have passion about your idea, in order to make your audiences think and feel and probe. There's no formula. You must travel untrodden paths, but always with open eyes and open mind.

Couch: Every one of your plays is related by this constant quality in terms of the *idea*, the *individual*. Yet each play has its own individuality.

Lee: Nena, I think that's one of the reasons we were so drawn to [American writer and leading world peace advocate who died in 1990] Norman Cousins (with whom we wrote *Whisper in the Mind*) and why we were so shaken by losing Norman. He had a quality-of-mind that I hope we have also: an enjoyment of life, an appreciation of the differences between people and the constructive interplay of those differences, the idea that living is a game, a contest which you sometimes win and sometimes lose. Out of that wonderful turmoil you find the real fun and laughter of living. . . .

Looking Forward, Not Back

Couch: Jerry, you once said that no one "has a platform that ultimately reaches more people" than the playwright. That's a sobering thought. How do you feel about the responsibility that places on you?

Lawrence: It's more important, we think, to be interesting than to be important.

Lee: If you're too worried about being "significant" what you write will be insignificant.

Lawrence: Or being "pertinent" turns out to be impertinent.

Lee: And being lofty turns out being downright dismal.

Lawrence: Nena, when I was [playwright] in residence [at Ohio State University] in Columbus a month or so ago, I was invited to conduct seminars at a dozen high school assemblies. Most of the students seemed bright, but generally "laid-back." I always read them "Grasses," the meadow scene in our *Thoreau* play: "Watch! Notice! Observe! . . . Did you ever have any *idea* so much was going on in Heywood's Meadow? I'll wager even Heywood doesn't know." And suddenly I felt they started to come awake, they were really watching, not merely keeping their eyes open, really listening. And by the end of each seminar, I sensed most of those students had begun to realize that the full life is living not just once, but a hundred times every minute, by absorbing with your pores and your souls, by daily roughing up your consciousness.

Lee: But writers who have a substantial body of work face a terrible danger—the "rear-view-mirror syndrome." We want to look forward, not back. Oh, it's wonderful that the Theatre Research Institute at Ohio State has been able to pull much of our work together and to give it a cohesion and an archival permanence. But Jerry and I must constantly be interested where the creative road is going, not where it's been, so we can hope to "shake up" the twenty-first century, too.

Lawrence: That's why we both teach and lecture all over the world. Because we feel the surest way to guarantee just a shred of immortality is to write, to teach, to have children. Now Bob's been luckier than I have, he's done all three; I don't have any physical, rock-them-to-sleep, shake-them-awake children. But then I say: Hey, wait a minute. All our plays are our children, too. And when our students write healthy, bouncing plays, that's like having grandchildren.

Couch: That's more than a shred of immortality.

Lee: We are so pleased that you're conducting this interview, Nena.

Lawrence: And everything you are doing at the Lawrence and Lee Theatre Research Institute is so important to us.

Lee: Do you know that for years nobody knew where Thoreau's actual draft of *Walden* was and what had become of his original notes? Finally they turned up in a box under his aunt's bed. I know how priceless those yellow foolscap pages are, neatly inscribed with a Thoreau pencil; I've held them in my hand at the Huntington Library in Pasadena. So many things get lost, unless there are dedicated people like you and [institute director] Alan Woods and all your staff to pull everything into perspective.

Lawrence: We're delighted that the editors have included in this issue [of *Studies in American Drama*] a bibliography of Lawrence and Lee works, and frankly, we're staggered at the long list of foreign translations of our plays.

Lee: I'm staggered at the things we have *yet* to write.

Inherit the Wind and Freedom of Thought

Inherit the Wind Establishes Firm Support for Freedom of Thought

David M. Galens and Lynn M. Spampinato

David M. Galens and Lynn M. Spampinato are editors of educational materials, many involving the theater.

The following essay by Galens and Spampinato discusses how Inherit the Wind *brings to the forefront a core conflict in the United States. On one side are those who firmly stand behind the separation of church and state; on the other are those who want religion to have as much say as science in public matters—especially in education. Although the playwrights used the* Scopes *trial, which addressed the teaching of the theory of evolution in schools, as inspiration for their story, the play is not history and is not, at its heart, about religion. Instead, it is about everyone's inherent right to think freely, especially during times of great change.*

In the blistering hot summer of 1925, two nationally-known legal minds, Clarence Darrow and William Jennings Bryan, battled in a tiny courtroom in Dayton, Tennessee, and, for a time, captured the attention of the world. The issue? A state law that forbade the teaching of evolution and a local teacher's violation of that law. The official name of this encounter was *Tennessee vs. John Thomas Scopes*, but it became known the world over as the *Scopes* "Monkey Trial."

Thirty years later, in 1955, playwrights Jerome Lawrence and Robert E. Lee published their dramatized version of the events of the summer of 1925. In a brief note at the beginning of the play, the playwrights admit that the *Scopes* Monkey Trial was clearly the inspiration for their work. But, the authors emphasize [that] "*Inherit the Wind* is not history" and that the "collision of Bryan and Darrow at Dayton was dramatic, but . . . not drama."

Bringing history to life through drama involves a risk that the central issues will be seen as "of the past" and of no relevance to the present. *Inherit the Wind*, however, has thrived for over three decades, suggesting an attraction for theatergoers far greater than that of a quaint look at America's past. As people search for meaning in an increasingly complex world, the different belief systems that attempt to provide some kind of understanding can, and do, come into conflict. Whether these systems wear such labels as religion, science, or politics, the struggles that exist within and between them is reflective of a cultural conflict that has yet to be, and may never be, resolved. *Inherit the Wind* then, is far more than the story of twelve exciting days in a Tennessee courtroom; it is a narrative of a nation and its people as they struggle to come to grips with the forces of change. . . .

The Right to Think

The Individual vs. the Machine. Jerome Lawrence said in an interview with Nena Couch [curator, Jerome Lawrence and Robert E. Lee Research Institute,] that "almost if not all of our plays share the theme of the dignity of every individual mind." The machine in this case is a combination of government and traditional thought, which are allied in *Inherit the Wind* to serve as adversaries against the right to think freely and exchange—or teach—those thoughts. In the exchange with [Matthew Harrison] Brady on the witness stand, [Henry] Drummond asks the witness if he believes a sponge thinks and if a man has the same privileges that a sponge does. When Brady responds in the affirmative, Drummond raises his voice for the first time and roars that his client "wishes to be accorded the same privileges as a sponge. He wishes to think." Drummond explores this idea further when he offers the supposition that "an un-Brady thought might still be holy." Drummond further illustrates his belief in the dignity of the individual mind after Brady's death when he asserts to [reporter E.K.] Hornbeck that Brady had just as much right to his strict religious views as the reporter does to his liberal ideals.

The idea of separation of church and state is as old as the American Republic itself, and it continues to be a source of controversy to this day. The central question of the play asks if the government, as represented by the city of Hillsboro and the laws of the state of Tennessee, should make decisions regarding what people can believe. Should one particular way of looking at the world be preferred over another? The question about the authority of the Bible also raises concerns: which translation or edition should be adopted as the "official" version of events? Drummond comments that the Bible is a good book—but not the only resource with which to view the world. God and religion are not the antagonists in *Inherit the Wind*, however, but merely provide the raw materials that people like Brady and Reverend Brown will use to combat Bert [Cate's] teaching of evolution. Like many lessons in blind faith, the play illustrates how unyielding devotion to a set of beliefs can lead a person to refute even the most obvious of truths. The play's optimism lies with Rachel and Bert, who, it is suggested, will find a balance between religion and science in their life together.

A New Way of Thinking

In 1925, the world was changing. Radio was beginning to replace the newspaper as a source of information. This, along with the widespread implementation of the telephone, provided a means for quickly relaying facts from one point to another. Technologies such as these brought new thought pro-

The Scopes *trial, which took place in this courtroom in Dayton, Tennessee, was an inspiration for Jerome Lawrence and Robert Edwin Lee's play* Inherit the Wind. © Underwood & Underwood/Corbis.

cesses to once-isolated rural towns, new ways of seeing and interpreting the world. There were enormous social changes taking place as well. Women had recently earned the right to vote, and many blacks were planting the seeds that would flower into the civil rights movement of the 1960s. To many people accustomed to a set way of life, these new developments presented a threat. One approach to dealing with this rapid change was to ignore it and retreat into their old, comfortable ways. When new modes of thinking threatened to change these traditions, people became uncomfortable, rejecting the "new" simply because it was not familiar. Not only did Bert's teaching of evolution represent a new way of thinking, to many it attacked the most sacred of all traditions, religion and thus their very way of life. Whereas many of the townfolk are fearful of this change, people like Brady and the Reverend resent it because it threatens their prosperity and power—the more people blindly believe, the easier they are to manipulate. Drummond's comment that maybe Brady had moved away by standing still illustrates how the prosecutor has profited from encouraging a stagnation of thought.

When Drummond tells the story of Golden Dancer, he outlines the characteristics of appearances and reality. A toy-store rocking horse, Golden Dancer's bright red mane, blue eyes, and golden color with purple spots dazzled the young Drummond. His parents worked extra and surprised him with the horse as a birthday present, and, when the excited boy jumped on the horse to ride, it broke in two. There was no substance to the object of Drummond's desire, only "spit and sealing wax." Drummond wants Cates, and by extension the audience of the play, to look closely at the arguments of people like Brady and Reverend Brown. They may have no more substance than Golden Dancer. . . .

This brief monologue [about the Golden dancer] suggests why Drummond takes on "unpopular" cases. "If something is a lie," Drummond tells Cates, "show it up for what it really is!" . . .

Historicity in *Inherit the Wind*

During the 1950s, America was in the process of settling in after the tumultuous years of World War II. But, beneath an air of prosperity and comfort, social tension existed. Lawrence and Lee sought to make some kind of sense of the climate of anxiety and fear fed by McCarthyism [a time of witch hunts for Communists led by Senator Joseph McCarthy] and anti-Communist sentiment. They found a parallel in the *Scopes* Monkey Trial [which ultimately deemed the teaching of evolution in public schools unlawful] of 1925. The story of *Inherit the Wind* is a dramatization, not a history lesson, as the playwrights make clear in their foreword to the play. It is a story about conflict in American culture.

Despite the play's overwhelming popularity, *Inherit the Wind*'s historical accuracy became an issue almost from the start. Those connected with the play itself (producers, directors, and other theater personnel) saw the *Scopes* Trial as a dramatic piece of history that could be made more dramatic by bringing it to the stage. Quoted on the University of Virginia's Web site, *American Studies*, Merle Debuskey, a promotional man behind the play, described the link between drama and factual events as "a vibrant, pulsating, slam-bang production, acclaimed by the critics as entertainment first and history by incidence." Another public relations firm, Daniel E. Lewitt Associates, called the play "living drama rather than a period piece" and said that "*Inherit the Wind* has significance to students because it illuminates a fragment of America's scholastic past [and] espouses important ideas dramatically."

On the other side of the issue, some had problems with *Inherit the Wind* as a history lesson for two reasons. First, there are significant discrepancies between the courtroom events of the play and the actual trial records. Even though Lawrence and Lee opened the play with a disclaimer, many viewed the play as a learning tool.

The other problem with using *Inherit the Wind* as historical documentation is the bias against the South that permeates the drama. The character of E.K. Hornbeck consistently refers to the South in less than flattering terms. Hornbeck longs to return to the North and escape the stultifying society of Hillsboro. Additionally, the play seems to suggest that the *Scopes* Monkey Trial is a southern failure and a sign of stagnation and ignorance. Drummond responds to Brady when asked why the two have moved so far apart: "Perhaps it is you who have moved away—by standing still." The Southerners, on the other hand, see Drummond and Hornbeck as intruders from the North. Drummond is referred to as "the gentleman from Chicago," a term not of respect but of scorn and derision.

Support of Freedom of Thought

In spite of these problems, Lawrence and Lee position them-selves firmly in support of freedom of thought and tolerance. Through Drummond, the playwrights try to establish a way for a culture or society to survive with its members holding differing beliefs. They support the importance of conflict and disagreement within a society, as well the idea that each posi-tion has its own merits and validity.

Whitney Bolton, in a *Morning Telegraph* review, said: "This is a play which, in the pleasant tasting icing of excellent the-atre, gets across to its audience the core of value beneath the icing: there is no more holy concept that the right of a man to think. . . . What is of importance is that from that musty little town . . . came a note of hope; that men could think of them-selves without censure or impoundment and that . . . the ac-cused made it easier, even though by only a fractional amount, for the next accused thinker to take his stand for it."

Inherit the Wind Found Tolerance in the Bible Belt

Kay Cattarulla

*Kay Cattarulla is a producer, writer, and director, who origi-
nated the literary series Selected Shorts: A Celebration of the
Short Story and created the award-winning literary series Arts &
Letters Live at the Dallas Museum of Art.*

*Many people, including authors Jerome Lawrence and Robert
Edwin Lee, were skeptical that* Inherit the Wind *would find a
receptive audience in Dallas, Texas, in the 1950s. A conservative,
religiously fundamentalist city, Dallas hardly seemed a place to
premiere a play about freedom of thought, especially one that involved religion. In the following article, however, Cattarulla reveals how the Bible Belt city embraced the play—a success that
helped lead the play to international fame. At the heart of the
play's success, contends Cattarulla, was its director in Dallas,
Margo Jones.*

In the summer of 1954, Margo Jones, the Dallas theater director, received a letter from her friend and play scout Jean
Baptiste "Tad" Adoue III. He had discovered a script, he told
her—a courtroom drama that had been submitted to eight
Broadway producers. All eight had turned it down, and the
authors, Jerome Lawrence and Robert E. Lee. had given up
hope for a production. Adoue thought the play would appeal
to, and challenge, Margo.

It "will take GUTS to do in the bible belt," he wrote. "It's
called INHERIT THE WIND."

Inherit the Wind did, in fact, receive its world premiere six
months later in Dallas (many would add "of all places"), the

Kay Cattarulla, "I'm Doing It, Darling," *Legacies: A History Journal for Dallas and
North Central Texas*, vol. 16, Fall 2004, pp. 39–47. Reproduced by permission.

conservative, fundamentalist stronghold that might have seemed like the last place where it could get a fair hearing. Nonetheless, the play landed in a city ideally suited to giving it a chance, thanks to four features that Dallas, perhaps alone among American cities of the mid-1950s, could put together: a professional theater, a director able to mold *Inherit the Wind*'s many scenes and characters into a powerhouse whole, a critic whose voice was heard and respected nationally, and an audience with an instinctive understanding of the material.

The production, which opened on January 10, 1955, launched a play that has since become world-famous. It was also Margo's last hurrah. . . .

An Idea Is a Great Monument

Lawrence and Lee had had one Broadway success in 1948, *Look Ma, I'm Dancin'! Inherit the Wind*, seemed unlikely to be their second.

The play was based on the 1925 *Scopes* "Monkey Trial" in Dayton, Tennessee, that tested the right of a high school teacher to introduce Darwin's Theory of Evolution into his classroom. The leads were based on the two real-life contending lawyers—the defense attorney Clarence Darrow and the God-invoking political orator William Jennings Bryan. Broadway producers had sensed box office poison in their long courtroom speech. In addition, the content was controversial.

But the play appealed to all Margo's instincts. She judged scripts intuitively ("I only know how to judge plays by goose flesh," she'd written to [playwright and novelist] William Inge in 1947), and she was determined to do this one. When she met the playwrights in New York, she greeted them with her favorite line from the play: "An idea is a greater monument than a cathedral." As she continued to quote their own words to them—". . . and the advancement of man's knowledge is more of a miracle than any sticks turned to snakes or the parting of the waters"—the authors realized that they had met a woman who shared their passion. As Jerome Lawrence said later, "Bob and I patted each other on the back, and said, 'here's our customer, this is quite a lady.'" Margo, too, sensed that a momentous partnership had been made. "You have certainly given me life through this script," she wrote to Lawrence and Lee.

Margo's enthusiasm, however, did not guarantee that *Inherit the Wind* would be appreciated in Dallas. Lawrence and Lee had written their drama as a protest against McCarthyism [the policy of finding and rooting out Communists in America led by Senator Joseph McCarthy] and the political repressions of the Cold War, and the city had taken a sharp turn to the right. Dallasite Bruce Alger was elected to Congress in November 1954 on a wave of anti-Communist rhetoric. In March 1955 a women's group, the Political Affairs Luncheon Club, would lead a campaign against the Dallas Museum of Fine Arts for keeping the work of "pinko" [Communist-leaning] artists in its collection. Over the next months, patriots would attack both the Museum and the Dallas Public Library for exhibiting work by known or suspected Communists such as [artists] Pablo Picasso, Louis Zorach, and Ben Shahn. Initially, the institutions gave ground to the protestors, and by the summer of 1955, Dallas would be drawing censure from the art world.

Premiering in the Bible Belt

A second touchy issue was the play's treatment of fundamentalist religion. Lawrence and Lee had used the *Scopes* Trial in the same way that playwright Arthur Miller evoked the Salem witchcraft trials in his drama *The Crucible*—as a metaphor for community hysteria that tries to silence dissident beliefs.

Alan Wood, Director of the Jerome Lawrence and Robert E. Lee Theatre Research Institute at Ohio State University, points out that "it's richly ironic that the play is now getting productions in response to efforts to mandate Creationism or

The 1955 debut of Jerome Lawrence and Robert Edwin Lee's play Inherit the Wind— *starring Tony Randall, Karl Light, and Paul Muni (right to left)—used the background of the historical* Scopes "Monkey" *trial to comment on the threats to freedom of thought present at the time.* Walter Sanders/Time Life Pictures/Getty Images.

Intelligent Design in public education. . . . Jerry and Bob purposefully selected the debate over evolution because it was settled and no longer controversial." They believed, says Wood, that the real anti-McCarthy message "would be crystal clear to mid-1950s audiences."

With both the political message and the treatment of religion likely to upset local sensitivities, a production in Dallas seemed risky. Tad Adoue's warning that it would take guts to stage the play there was echoed by the authors' own agent, Harold Freedman. "Margo, you don't want to do this play. Everybody will—will crucify you down there in the Bible belt," Freedman told her over the phone. Margo replied, "I'm doing it, darling." . . .

The Audience and the Critic

Margo kept excellent records (the Dallas Public Library's Margo Jones Collection is packed with business files, correspondence, scripts, photographs, clippings, memorabilia, and much more), but she lived before the age of the audience survey.

We can surmise, however, that, like Margo herself, many who attended her theater had come from small town or rural backgrounds. Some had been transformed into rich, well-dressed theater patrons with money recently earned from oil, cotton, real estate, and banking. In his memoir *In the New World: Growing Up with America from the Sixties to the Eighties*, Lawrence Wright describes Dallas, where he grew up, as a city "self created like no other." But for all their forward-looking optimism and tendency to ignore the past, many Dallasites of the 1950s had roots in small, religious communities similar to the play's fictional Hillsboro.

This alone would guarantee Margo an involved audience for *Inherit the Wind*, and there were other strands in Dallas history and society that were on her side.

The city had a progressive tradition, as exemplified by the Civic Federation, founded as early as 1917 as a forum for continuing education, cultural programs, and political discussions. Margaret Sanger, the crusader for birth control, the socialist Norman Thomas, and labor advocate Max Eastman had all spoken there, along with black educator Booker T. Washington, biologist Julian Huxley, and philosopher Bertrand Russell.

Dallas also loved pleasure and entertainment—even today Dallas audiences are regarded as "hot" in theater parlance: eager to laugh and respond. Large crowds flocked to the vaudeville houses lining Elm Street early in the century and attended the same theaters when they were transformed into movie palaces in the 1920s. The highly successful amateur Dallas Little Theatre had built a theater tradition from the 1920s to the early 1940s. Dallasites also loved the State Fair—educational but entertaining, with a history of tantalizing spectacles such as the Apple Dance offered by M[ademoise]lle

Corinne (a native Texan) at the 1936 Texan Centennial. In a contemporary newsreel, she appears to have performed totally in the nude. Enjoying its own history as a wide-open town, Dallas was said to have always had "a soft spot for a high class hustler."

Above all other factors favorable to *Inherit the Wind*. Dallas had John Rosenfield, the nationally renowned critic of *The Dallas Morning News*. Rosenfield, more than any other individual, built the cultural institutions of Dallas, and he ran its artistic life with an iron hand. Thanks to Rosenfield, *Time* magazine wrote, culture in Dallas bloomed "like a rose on the dry plains." Rosie himself had brought Margo to Dallas to open a professional theater. He supported her beliefs and theater philosophy; although he handed out bad notices freely when her productions disappointed him. He was well qualified to judge the merits of *Inherit the Wind*, and his opinion would be heard.

Involving the Audience in the Scenes

In December 1954, Jerome Lawrence arrived at Love Field [Dallas's airport] to attend rehearsals. Margo met him, newsreel cameras in tow. Lawrence looks youthful and shy in WBAP Channel 5's archival footage. Margo, who had appeared aged and unfocused a month earlier at a luncheon in her honor at the Adolphus [Hotel], looks rejuvenated. Co-author Lee arrived soon after to work with Margo and the cast.

The long courtroom speeches that Broadway producers believed would empty seats were thrilling and gripping to Margo. She dramatized them by placing extras who enacted the jury members on the stairs that separated the sections of the theater. As lawyers directed their arguments into the house, the audience felt that it was sitting in judgment. The small stage and the nearness of the audience on all four sides worked to heighten the intensity of the play. The action engulfed the spectators, as Margo intended.

She was equally inventive in the Prayer Meeting scene. Again she placed actors on the stairs, this time as church members. Margo told the cast to seek out and watch Holy Rollers services to prepare for playing the scene—to be ready for "a lot of body movement and a lot of singing." The music was created by stage manager Fred Hoskins, who was raised in a fundamentalist church in Fort Worth. Hoskins procured a drum to lead the actors onto the stage for the revival meeting, and as [actress] Harriet Slaughter recalls, "We came out marching, singing 'Follow the Fold.'"

During rehearsals, according to Lawrence, "Margo got dead center and was the Preacher . . . to have the cast imbibe this, and my God it worked! During the performance, audiences were like part of the Prayer Meeting. They'd see someone in the aisle stand up and shout a Hosannah, and they'd stand up and shout a Hosannah." The wilderness and excitement are still vivid to [Lee's wife] Janet Lee, who told us she has never seen the equal of Margo's staging of the prayer meeting. In the words of journalist Patsy Swank, the scene came "straight out of Margo's past, and straight out of the past of so many of us that were born in this part of the country and knew a lot about the importance of really functional religion."

Both authors doubted that the production would be successful. Janet Lee, arriving for the opening, was met at the airport by her husband, who told her repeatedly, "It's a disaster." Lawrence was so tense and exclaimed, "I can't stand it," so many times, that Margo finally suggested, "Well, Darling, why don't you just leave?"

Dallas Welcomes Free Speech

On opening night, January 10, Margo greeted the audience at the door as she always did. The sell-out crowd in black tie, furs, and jewels was completely riveted by the play, watching entranced, some joining in the excitement during the prayer meeting. As for the anger that many thought would be unleashed by a play preaching free speech and the dignity of the human mind in the Bible belt, no complaint was registered.

The company, the authors, and Margo went back to her apartment at the Stoneleigh Hotel to await reviews, which came in late that night. Lawrence has described Margo kicking off her shoes and reading the notices aloud with tears running down her cheeks.

Virgil Meiers in *The Dallas Times Herald* wrote that "Margo Jones directed Theatre '55 through its first premiere of 1955 ... lighting up a brilliant play.... Theatrical sparks flew ... making the burning issue of the right to think sizzle and explode again. It is simply one of the best plays Miss Jones has staged at her theatre, and one of the best productions she has given to a play."

Rosenfield wrote, "A new play of power, humanity, and universal truth found its way into Margo Jones's Theatre '55 ... one of the proudest productions of our unusual theatre." He compared the playwrights to [George Bernard] Shaw and [Henrik] Ibsen. He further pleased Lawrence and Lee by realizing that the part of the journalist Hornbeck was written in iambic pentameter.

New York inquiries began as soon as the reviews came out. The Broadway production was acquired by Herman Shumlin, one of the eight producers who had initially turned the play down. *Inherit the Wind* opened at the National Theater on April 26, 1955, directed by Shumlin, and produced "in association with Margo Jones." Margo received her producing credit by virtue of having raised a significant portion of the budget, but Shumlin shut her out of any creative role in the production.

The play was a hit—as John Rosenfield had wryly predicted. It would do well in New York, Rosenfield said because it "depicted the South that New Yorkers love, the South of tape worm, ignorance and bigotry." ...

The Broadway production, starring Paul Muni and Ed Begley, ran for three years, and the play was made into a successful movie with Spencer Tracy and Frederic March. It was revived for the Broadway stage in 1996 ad has appeared in three television versions. It continues to be performed all over the world and has been translated into thirty languages.

Remembering Dallas and Director Jones

Robert E. Lee says: "Margo saw in *Inherit the Wind* the conflict and the drama which not one other person in the American theater saw. . . . As a result of this experiment in Texas, Jerry and I realized that theater must be allowed to escape from the little bird cage in mid-town Manhattan. . . . Broadway could not originate its own plays . . . they should be created on the Texas Fair Grounds, or in Louisville or the Long Wharf [Theatre in New Haven, Connecticut]."

Margo's vision and courage could have had no more eloquent tribute. She, however, never saw the national theater movement that her work helped to start. On July 24, 1955, she died as the result of a bizarre poisoning accident suffered in her apartment at the Stoneleigh. Headlines such as "Good Night, Sweet Tornado," national and local obituaries, and a stream of telegrams from theater celebrities attest to the shock of her death, at the age of 43, and to the value of her brief life.

Her theater struggled on for four years, then closed in 1959. Margo's reputation began to fade, Jerome Lawrence and Robert E. Lee, joined by Tad Adoue, established the Margo Jones award in her memory. Every year since 1961, the award has gone to an individual who has performed outstanding service to the theater. Eugene and Margaret McDermott provided funds to build SMU's [Southern Methodist University's] Margo Jones Theater in 1969. A second theater bearing her name was inaugurated at her alma mater, Texas Woman's University in Denton, in 1982. A plaque describing Margo's achievements is now displayed in her hometown of Livingston, where she is buried in the Jones family plot.

"We always say we were born in Dallas as playwrights," Jerome Lawrence observed. On January 10, 2005, the fiftieth anniversary of *Inherit the Wind*'s world premiere in Fair Park, the city that had been expected to end the play's chances for good can be excused for taking a self-congratulatory bow.

How *Inherit the Wind* Shaped History and Thought

Gad Guterman

Gad Guterman is the education director of the Vineyard Theatre in New York City.

Jerome Lawrence and Robert Edwin Lee, in their introduction to Inherit the Wind, *point out that the play is not history. Guterman disagrees with the idea that the play and history are not closely interwoven. In the following selection, Guterman discusses not only how history impacted* Inherit the Wind, *but also how* Inherit the Wind *impacted history. The playwrights intended the play to be a celebration of freedom of thought in general, but as the Christian Right has gained more political power, the play has increasingly been viewed as a specific defense of the theory of evolution.*

*I*nherit the Wind "is theatre," write Lawrence and Lee in their opening note to the published script. Distancing themselves from the actual *Scopes* trial, the playwrights explicitly attempt to contain their work within a specific field: it "does not pretend," they continue, to be anything other than a play. But *Inherit the Wind* has not been contained within the artistic field; like a ghost that moves through walls, the piece has entered new spaces, one of which is the legal universe. It is not *just* theatre.

To begin, the ghosts of the *Scopes* trial haunt *Inherit the Wind*. For this reason, the play can never fully break ties with the legal field that offered the seed idea for the project. The events that occurred in Dayton, Tennessee, during the sum-

Gad Guterman, "Field Tripping: The Power of Inherit the Wind," *Theatre Journal*, vol. 60, December 2008, pp. 571–78. Copyright © 2008, University and College Theatre Association of the American Theatre Association. Reproduced by permission of The Johns Hopkins University Press.

mer of 1925 prove especially complex in this analysis; the court case—centering on a teacher's right to teach evolution in a school system that explicitly prohibited such teaching—served from the beginning as a legal proceeding-cum-entertainment. That the Radio Man in the play segues from the [character Bert] Cates case to the Matinee Musicale smartly captures the position that the *Scopes* courtroom drama held in 1925. As the first-ever trial to be broadcast over the radio in the United States, the events in Dayton captured the popular imagination in unprecedented ways. Numbers might again serve as a straightforward means to illustrate the trial's popularity: twenty-two telegraphers transmitted about 165,000 words daily to recipients throughout the country and across the Atlantic; and over a hundred newspaper reporters invaded the small town during the trial, with more words being dispatched about the case than on any other analogous event in US history.

Such notoriety implies that the case itself was "haunted"—adding a new layer of phantasmal density if we consider [author of *When Law Goes Pop: The Vanishing Line Between Law and Popular Culture*] Richard Sherwin's use of that term to describe famous trials. Sherwin explains that popular trials necessarily function on several signifying levels simultaneously and turn specific legal controversies into larger symbols. The highly mediated event turned individuals into ideas and personified institutions. [Author of *Popular Trials*] Robert Hariman observes that notorious trials are typified by patent character studies of each of players so that the issues at hand can be easily attached and judged according to a particular personality: "substitution of the speaker for the speech" he calls it. Therefore, although opposing counselors William Jennings Bryan and Clarence Darrow were already noted public figures when they arrived in Dayton, the press's portrayal of them during the trial transformed them into personifications of fundamentalism and agnosticism, respectively. As subjects of newspaper stories and cartoons, as radio voices and personages, and as public orators, their specificity as agents in the legal field dissipated while they seeped into other discourses and fields. "Radio! God, this is going to break down a lot of walls," utters Drummond sagely in the play when he first sees the microphone in the courtroom, thereby acknowledging that as the trial metamorphoses into both journalism and show business—that is, as one field bleeds into other fields—social structures and our conceptions of them must necessarily change.

Inherit the Wind Shaped History

Inherit the Wind, which Lawrence and Lee insist "is not history"—again striving to constrain the play's position within the field of theatre—cannot escape its historical inspiration. Despite the playwrights' denial, history has always nourished the theatre. [Author of *The Haunted Stage: The Theatre as Memory Machine*] Marvin Carlson argues that theatre—"the most haunted of human cultural structures"—operates as a simulacrum [image] for the historiographic process, and in many ways proves to be a most effective "repository of cultural memory." It allows for ghosts to return to the world of the living, for histories to be quite literally re-membered as the past takes material shape in a present stage. In the bodies of actors Ed Begley and Paul Muni, the ghosts of William Jennings Bryan and Clarence Darrow did manage to resurface— sort of. Carlson reminds us that ghosts can be tricky, that our encounter with them results in shifts and modifications of memory. *Inherit the Wind* quite clearly demonstrates how the legal history of the *Scopes* trial can be altered and re-imagined by something that is "not history" but a mere play.

Indeed, unlike *The Bird of Paradise* [a play by Richard Walton Tully that premiered on Broadway in 1912], which after about twenty years following its appearance did drop into an ostensible historical dustbin, *Inherit the Wind* has actively shaped history. [Author of *Summer for the Gods*] Edward Larson explains, in his study of the *Scopes* trial and the continuing debate over evolution, that *Inherit the Wind* has proven much more influential than the real-life trial proceedings in shaping how the case has come to be interpreted, despite key differences between the historical record and the play's fiction: "It may not have been accurate history, but it was brilliant theater—and it all but replaced the actual trial in the nation's memory." Especially after the movie version was released in 1960—sparking a broad popularity that the original theatrical product by itself probably could not have achieved—the general public has substituted the fictional Matthew Harrison Brady for Bryan, Henry Drummond for Darrow, and Bertram Cates for John Scopes. *Inherit the Wind*'s biased and exaggerated version of the Darrow-Bryan courtroom confrontation has gained acceptance as an accurate retelling of the legal event, and as such, it has gained power as a legal symbol with the type of "prominent cultural presence" that [authors of *The Common Place of Law: Stories from Everyday Life*] Patricia Ewick and Susan Silbey note serves to structure our experience and understanding of the law. We could say that history now performs the play, not the other way around.

A Cultural Production

[In "Two Stories of the Scopes Trial"] Lawrence Bernabo and Celeste Condit agree that *Inherit the Wind* has "probably provided most Americans with most of their 'knowledge' about the Scopes trial," and offer that the "impact of the play/film/television movie can be found even in academia." They note that only after the Broadway production did the trial receive an entry in the *Encyclopedia Britannica* (although thirty years had passed since the incredibly well-publicized "monkey trial"), and that some college history textbooks draw on the more exciting stage battle to describe the slightly less charged courtroom confrontation. Even law professors Paul Bergman and Michael Asimow, who in their *Reel Justice* attempt to highlight some of the legal incongruities of popular culture's dealing with the law, introduce *Inherit the Wind* by telling us, inaccurately, that it is "enthralling to watch Clarence Darrow and William Jennings Bryan come to life as they square off . . . in the story of the Scopes Monkey Trial." There is thus no acknowledgment of Lawrence and Lee's attempt at fiction—instead, a collapse of the *real* into the *reel*.

This slippage from legal story to theatrical/cinematic representation is so pervasive that it almost becomes naturalized, often being taken for granted. Kary Doyle Smout [in *The Creation/Evolution Controversy: A Battle for Cultural Power*] touts *Inherit the Wind* as a "most influential representation of the Scopes Trial," but expunges the arts from his list of participants in the creation/evolution controversy: the debate, he tells us, "involves a broad range of disciplines, including anthropology, biology, geology, history, law, paleontology, philosophy, religion, sociology, and theology." Given his commentary about the play, it is quite remarkable that he does not include any sort of artistic discourse in his introduction. His study of the debate as a rhetorical phenomenon ably posits that what has always been at stake for both evolutionists and fundamentalists is the authority to define terminology, to use language and representation as weapons to overcome opponents. Although he treats *Inherit the Wind* as an important element in the debate, Smout fails to follow through with his ideas—for example, writing that Darrow's cross-examination of Bryan during the trial "has become legendary," but leaving the process of immortalization as an obvious fact. *Inherit the Wind*'s popularity is here simply assumed, and Smout never questions how a legend comes to be made or how the field of cultural production provides the necessary mechanisms for popularity to be achieved. Neither does Marjorie Garber [in "Cinema Scopes: Evolution, Media, and the Law"] consider the artistic field as part of the "peculiar confluence of religion, science, public education, and law" surrounding the *Scopes* trial and its legacy. Even though the film version of the play is at the center of her study, and audiences' perceptions of *Inherit the Wind* underpin her argument, the arts ultimately disappear from the issues that Garber thinks significant: "[a]cademic freedom, local option, religion in the schools, prayer in the courtroom" are of central concern, while cultural production seems merely to service these issues—not to matter in and of itself.

A Blurred Line

Interestingly, at times both Smout and Garber describe the *Scopes* case in relation to *Inherit the Wind*, not the other way around. Garber is compelled to introduce Scopes as "the 'Bert Cates' of *Inherit the Wind*," as if the name Scopes fails to mean as much on its own, even for her ostensibly well-educated audience. Smout, who is explicitly analyzing questions of language and representation, falls captive to the misperceptions that *Inherit the Wind* has perpetuated. Thus he, too, introduces Scopes quite tersely (and imprecisely) as "a high school science teacher," only to correct himself pages later and explain that "he was actually a coach at the high school who thought he had only taught Darwin once as a substitute teacher . . . and was uncertain later whether he had actually ever taught the subject." The initial five words are, admittedly, a minor inaccuracy, perhaps even negligible, but nonetheless describe Bertram Cates and not John Scopes, thus attesting to the power of popular culture to replace real-life players with fictionalized characters in the social imagination. The already-mediated roles that Bryan, Darrow, and Scopes came to play during the trial have undoubtedly been remolded by the legacy of *Inherit the Wind*. Other major participants in the 1925 case—such as defense attorney Dudley Field Malone, who on several occasions stole Bryan's and Darrow's spotlight—have been easily forgotten in the popular imagination, since they lack a major counterpart in *Inherit the Wind*. As Scopes has metamorphosed from a sports coach with no substantive knowledge of evolution into a science teacher/hero determined to educate his students, so has Bryan been transformed in the public imagination into the quintessence of conservatism and fundamentalism. Smout aptly notes that now "[s]tatements about Bryan's socialism [and liberalism] usually come as a surprise." Indeed, it is virtually impossible to recount the hundreds of instances in which the boundary between fictional and historical figure is blurred, if not altogether eliminated.

Bernabo and Condit aver at the beginning of their essay that the *Scopes* case

> continues to symbolize the dominant American consensus about the legitimate roles of religion and science in national life. The trial stands as a potent cultural image of the boundaries between science and religion because, as a special type of legal event, it provided the locus for the negotiation between these powerful, competing social forces.

While they suggest in closing that *Inherit the Wind* has become a sort of substitute for the actual trial, they also, like Smout, do not carry the argument to its logical conclusion. If *Inherit the Wind* provides the popular version of the events in Dayton, then it is the play and not the *Scopes* trial itself that today stands as the potent cultural image. . . .

Given *Inherit the Wind*'s participation in a continuing and heated debate (the legal battles persist to this day; even presidential candidates in 2007 and 2008 were asked whether they believe in evolution!), it is its ghosts and not those of the *Scopes* trial proper that seem to haunt many Christian conservatives. While [conservative syndicated columnist and author] Ann Coulter's arguments are certainly extremist, her recent [2006] book *Godless* does capture *Inherit the Wind*'s very material effects on present-day culture: "Liberals act as if they have to maintain a constant vigil against the coming theocracy in America because of what happened in *Inherit the Wind*." What happened *in* the play/movie is the work of artists, and so it is the cultural product rather than the events in Dayton that seems to spark action on both sides of the debate. Coulter rightly notes that the movie has become a staple of middle- and upper-school curricula across the country, and, in what may be a first, she would probably agree with [astronomer and author] Carl Sagan's view that *Inherit the Wind* has proven more influential than the trial itself in defending our right to question and investigate what life is. Larson maintains that *Inherit the Wind*, and not the trial, continues to motivate creationists to rally against those promoting evolution in the schools. Therefore the cultural product has not merely been absorbed into the ongoing battle over teaching evolution in schools, it still actively fuels the dispute.

A Changing Role in Evolution Debate

There are, to be sure, politics behind the power of ghosts, and it is critical to address the question of who controls the means of producing and disseminating popular cultural products. We might attribute the energy and fluidity with which *Inherit the Wind* haunts the ongoing debate over evolution to the entertainment industry's ostensible liberal bias; the play and its subsequent filmed incarnations display a liberal proclivity when it comes to scientific thinking, as they stand up for "the individual human mind," which Drummond so passionately defends, and for our right to think freely. The 1960 movie, for one, exemplifies the "creeping leftism" that came to dominate the New Hollywood of the 1960s, and as noted above, even its premiere proved a significant political occasion. That *Inherit the Wind* now reaches deeper into our collective consciousness than what actually occurred in Dayton could therefore be read as the victory of a liberal cultural machinery successfully attacking religious fundamentalism. This is Coulter's contention in *Godless*.

Although we must be wary of easy categorizations, and although the label of "liberal" does not neatly describe a piece that propagates and replicates traditionally oppressive images of the South, the poor, and women, it is certainly the case that the religious fundamentalists caricatured in *Inherit the Wind* had considerably less power to control the media during the 1950s and 1960s than they do today. The play's popularity flourished precisely during a period in which its most blatant targets did not enjoy the type of political presence and concentration necessary to garner a broad cultural reach. As the Christian Right has strengthened its political activism and successfully championed an accompanying cultural upheaval, the role of *Inherit the Wind* within the debate over evolution has changed and continues to change.

With religious fundamentalism standing in for McCarthyism [anti-Communist sentiment and legal action in the 1950s], it is possible that when the play premiered, the question of whether men came from apes really was "beside the point," as the character of Rachel admits. [Actor] Tony Randall, the original E.K. Hornbeck [the journalist character in *Inherit the Wind*], believed the play would not even be taken seriously at the time, given that in 1955 the religious Right seemed to him nothing more than "a lunatic fringe." Not so in 1996, when Randall, as artistic director of the National Actors Theatre, headed the first Broadway revival: "The play is one-thousand times more pertinent today," he explained. And of the 2007 revival, which had present-day audience members sitting on-stage as spectators of the 1925 proceedings, [*New York Times* critic] Ben Brantley noted that such blurring of the "then" and the "now" aptly emphasized that "the subject of teaching evolution and religion in public schools is even more topical today than it was ... more than half a century ago." Increasingly, then, *Inherit the Wind* is viewed specifically as a defense of evolutionary theory rather than as a general commentary on freedom of thought. And today, opponents of evolution must contend not only with scientific evidence that seems to support the theory, but also with a popular product like *Inherit the Wind*, which has quite effectively seeped into our cultural consciousness. Perhaps to combat such a pervasive reach, these opponents might, given their ever-increasing power to control the means of cultural production, develop a new piece that can fictionalize and eventually replace the history of *Inherit the Wind*. The difficulty in this . . . is that *Inherit the Wind* plays a role even in what are supposed to be the more powerful fields in our society. Crucially, *Inherit the Wind* has entered the legal field.

Inherit the Wind Distorts Reality and Possibility

Carol Iannone

Carol Iannone is editor at large for the scholarly journal Academic Questions and writes about literature and culture.

In the following selection, Iannone details how the historical in-accuracies of Inherit the Wind *have damaged people's views of the* Scopes *trial of 1925, which determined the teaching of evolution in public schools to be illegal, and of all those involved in the trial. More importantly, Iannone believes the play's distortion of facts has caused damage to antievolutionists' arguments, the core of which is that evolution is no more fact than is any religious belief. Although the play's central theme is freedom of thought—based upon the choice between bigotry and enlightenment—some critics see the play as promoting reverse bigotry.*

While *Inherit the Wind* remains faithful to the broad outlines of the historical events it portrays, it flagrantly distorts the details, and neither the fictionalized names nor the cover of artistic license can excuse what amounts to an ideologically motivated hoax. The film, for example, depicts [teacher Bert] Cates arrested in the act of teaching evolution by a grim posse of morally offended citizens, while in fact no effort was made to enforce the Butler Act [a Tennessee law prohibiting teachers from denying the biblical account of human creation]. What actually brought the issue to light—never mentioned in play or film—was that the American Civil Liberties Union advertised for someone to challenge the law. Several Dayton citizens, hoping the publicity would benefit their town, approached [John] Scopes as a possible candidate.

Scopes was actually a mathematics teacher and athletic coach and had only briefly substituted as a biology teacher. He did not remember teaching evolution, but he had used the standard textbook, Hunter's *Civic Biology*, which contained a short section on the subject. Scopes was surprised to hear how relatively knowledgeable the student witnesses were, and he speculated that they must have picked up what they knew somewhere else and come to associate it with his class. Scopes himself knew little beyond the rudiments, and the defense thought it best to keep him off the stand, where his lack of knowledge (not to mention his uncertainty as to whether he had taught the subject) might prove embarrassing. . . .

A Purely Fabricated Plot

The essential plot elements of *Inherit the Wind*—the lonely stand of the brave individualist against the small-minded bigotry of the townspeople, Cates' fear and trembling as he waits in his prison cell, the threat of ruin hanging over his head ("The Scopes character and his fiancee play each scene as if he were on the way to the electric chair," wrote one film reviewer)—are pure fabrication. Far from living in fear, Scopes went swimming during one hot lunchtime recess with two of the young assistant prosecutors (including [prosecutor William Jennings] Bryan's son). The reprimand Scopes received from defense attorney [Arthur Garfield] Hays when they were late getting back to the courtroom may have been the roughest treatment he received.

So, too, *Inherit the Wind* distorts its Bryan figure. The play does allow a certain benignity, color, and agility to the man, if only to give [defense lawyer Henry] Drummond a worthy adversary, but in many ways it belittles him. Years after the trial, the playwrights met with Hays, who may have influenced their picture of Bryan. But many journalistic accounts even at the time depicted a past-his-prime Bryan trailing clouds of fundamentalist ignorance and, like [character Matthew Harrison] Brady, squirming in distress on the witness stand under his adversary's questioning.

Many reporters seemed to share the prejudices of [commentator H.L.] Mencken, who ridiculed Bryan in print as "a tinpot pope in the coca-cola belt." The historian R.M. Cornelius, who has written a great deal on the *Scopes* Trial, reports, "A review of the trial press coverage reveals that the typical newsman had both an ear for a good story and a mouth hungry for Bryan's blood." One reporter never even attended the trial sessions, remarking, "I don't have to know what's going on; I know what my paper wants me to write." During the famous cross-examination by [historical defense lawyer Clarence] Darrow only six reporters were present; the others were taking a long lunch, thinking that the most important portions of the trial had passed. (Scopes later helped the absentee reporters file their stories.) The number of reporters dwindled during the trial, and even Mencken did not stay through the whole eight days.

Bryan's True Biblical Beliefs

A review of the actual transcript reveals that Bryan was often exuberant, funny, discerning, and focused during the trial. It also shows, contrary to *Inherit the Wind*, that he was familiar with [evolution theorist Charles] Darwin, and may even have understood the evolutionary doctrine better than his adversaries, or at least had a better idea of what was really at stake. He did have some embarrassing moments during the ninety minutes of Darrow's relentless questioning, but he often gave as good as he got.

Bryan was not a biblical literalist. He volunteered to Darrow—it was not wormed out of him, as the play suggests—that the "days" in the biblical account of creation were not twenty-four hour days; he cited Genesis 2:4, in which the word "generations" seems to be used as a substitute for "days."

He did not insist that the "sun stood still" in Joshua 10:13, but explained that the Bible was using the language of the time. At the same time he did not yield on his belief in miracles and the primacy of divine power. If his supporters felt disappointment over Bryan's testimony—the play makes much of the crowd's turning on him—it was not because he looked stupid as a defender of crude fundamentalism, but because he wasn't a defender of crude fundamentalism.

The Real Developments of the Trial

Bryan's real mistake was to take the stand at all, but he seemed to feel he had to accept Darrow's challenge to testify or implicitly admit the indefensibility of his position, and he later felt that he had at least stood his ground. "These gentlemen," he said on the stand, "came here to try revealed religion. I am here to defend it, and they can ask me any questions they please." For his part, Darrow realized that neither the constitutionality of the Butler Act nor the truth of evolution could be settled in Dayton, but he relished the publicity he could gain for his cause: "Preventing bigots and ignoramuses from controlling the education of the United States," as he memorably put it.

But it is certainly not true that Bryan and his beliefs were crushed in Dayton. Scopes himself, even while sporadically trying to render a portrait of a broken man, remarked that the Great Commoner [Bryan] seemed amazingly buoyant during the trial, always remaining "the exuberant Bryan who could survive any defeat." And while the antievolutionary cause may have suffered embarrassment, the guilty verdict was overturned a year later only on a technicality. Several state laws similar to the Butler Act were not declared unconstitutional until 1968.

It is true that Bryan was not able to deliver the lengthy closing statement he considered his life's "mountain peak," but not because the judge cut short the trial. Rather, after the

In this scene from the 1960 film based on the play Inherit the Wind, *E.K. Hornbeck (Gene Kelly), Rachel Brown (Donna Anderson), Bertram T. Cates (Dick York), and Henry Drummond (Spencer Tracy) participate in the courtroom battle of beliefs and of intellectual freedom based on the* Scopes *"Monkey" trial.* © Bettmann/Corbis.

cross-examination of Bryan (which was stricken from the record the following day), Darrow stated his willingness to accept a guilty verdict in order to move to appeal. This obviated the need for closing statements. Darrow later admitted that the defense had purposely wanted to deprive Bryan of his closing statement for fear of his legendary oratorical powers.

Moreover, Bryan did not have a mortal stroke in the courtroom, but died five days after the trial. His death may have been due partly to exhaustion and stress, but he also suffered from a diabetic condition that he did not carefully watch. He passed away peacefully during an afternoon nap and after a heavy meal. (The irreverent line spoken by the cynical Hornbeck at Brady's death—"He died of a busted belly"—was actually Darrow's private remark on hearing that Bryan had died.) But as historian Lawrence W. Levine puts it, if Bryan was destroyed by the trial, "he did a masterly job of concealing it during the five days of life remaining to him." Bryan took heart in the legal victory and set himself to the fight with renewed vigor. He traveled, gave speeches, and arranged for publication of the address he had not been permitted to deliver. Scopes himself denied that the trial killed Bryan, though perhaps because he did not want his side to bear the onus.

Even in small things, *Inherit the Wind* goes out of its way to diminish Bryan. Drummond derides the honorary title of "Colonel" that Hillsboro bestows upon Brady, protesting, "I am not familiar with Mr. Brady's military record." In fact, Bryan had been a colonel in the U.S. Army during the Spanish-American War (though he never saw combat). The play's Brady is mothered by a wife who cradles him in her bosom, murmuring, "Baby, Baby," though Bryan's wife was actually a semi-invalid of whom he was protective and solicitous.

The Battle of Two Types of Mind

These systematic alterations serve a single, obvious end: to ridicule Bryan and his followers for their backwardness and religious prejudice. The stage directions instruct, "It is important to the concept of the play that the town is visible always, looming there, as much on trial as the individual defendant." The thinker is in jail, while the "morons" (as Mencken called them) roam free—led by Brady, "the idol of all Morondom" (as Darrow later termed Bryan). The stage directions indicate the time of the play as "Not too long ago," and the playwrights' note—always included in any production's program—declares ominously, "It might have been yesterday. It could be tomorrow." The trial, as Arthur Garfield Hays put it, "was a battle between two types of mind—the rigid, orthodox, accepting, unyielding, narrow, conventional mind, and the broad, liberal, critical, cynical, skeptical, and tolerant mind."

But was it really so simple? Since much of Bryan's political progressivism is in keeping with the playwrights' own views, they split the Bryan figure in two—the "enlightened" progressive champion of the common man versus the "bigoted" religious fundamentalist. Drummond, who had supported Brady in two of his presidential bids (as Darrow had supported Bryan in real life), says at Brady's death, "A giant once lived in that body. But Matt Brady got lost. Because he was looking for God too high up and too far away." In fact, the two sides of Bryan, the democratic and the religious, were complementary. According to historian LeRoy Ashby, Bryan was sustained by "the combined heritages of evangelical faith and the republicanism of the nation's revolutionary era." The democracy he worked for was built upon "the virtuous citizen," and he worried that Darwinism "would cause people to lose a sense of God's presence. . . . It justified an economic jungle and 'discourages those who labor for the improvement of man's condition.'" Convinced as he was that belief in God and in man's spiritual nature was vital to human progress and a just social order, Bryan was troubled by numerous reports he had received of young people who had lost their faith under the tutelage of skeptical, even atheistic, professors. Bryan believed in separation of church and state, but, according to Ashby, he felt such stories of lost faith indicated "that the state was in fact teaching against religion, and that atheists and evolutionists were enjoying something against which democratic reformers had long battled—special privileges."

Although *Inherit the Wind* presents a Bryan torn by fear of change, it was actually Darrow who was caught in contradictions. Darrow was an agnostic determinist—the play's suggestion that Drummond may be "more religious" than Brady is another fabrication—who believed that human beings are driven by forces beyond their control. Yet in the *Scopes* Trial he defended the individual mind and freedom of thought. Darrow's questions to Scopes' students—"Did it hurt you any?", Do you "still believe in church although you were told all life comes from a single cell?" (the play adds "Haven't murdered anybody since breakfast?")—were simply disingenuous. One year earlier, Darrow had defended Nathan Leopold and Richard Loeb, two brilliant university students who murdered a boy for the intellectual experience of committing the perfect crime. At Dayton, Bryan read out Darrow's famous excuse for the earlier defendants: "Is there any blame attached because somebody took [nineteenth-century German philosopher Friedrich] Nietzsche's philosophy seriously and fashioned his life on it? . . . Your Honor, it is hardly fair to hang a nineteen-year-old boy for the philosophy that was taught him at the university." As [literary scholar] Richard Weaver commented on Bryan's use of the Leopold and Loeb record: "To Darrow's previous position that the doctrine of Nietzsche is capable of immoral influence, Bryan responded that the doctrine of evolution is likewise capable of immoral influence."

Are Religion and Evolution Compatible?

Both the play and the movie version of *Inherit the Wind* vastly oversimplify religion's relation to evolution. The play insists that there is no contradiction between Christianity and Darwinism. "It is only a matter of the method He has chosen in creation," Maynard M. Metcalf, a zoologist from Oberlin College, declared in expert testimony permitted at the trial (though not before the jury). As the play's Cates puts it, "Living comes from a long miracle, it didn't just happen in seven days." The defense, both actual and fictional, wanted to isolate an ignorant, biblical literalism as the only kind of religion that disputes evolution. And, indeed, they have been joined in this view by many mainstream religious leaders in the seventy years since. This understanding has been challenged more recently, however, by such credible figures as Phillip E. Johnson of the University of California, and William B. Provine, an historian of science from Cornell. A leading adherent of Darwinian evolution, Provine has observed that "prominent evolutionists have joined with equally prominent theologians and religious leaders to sweep under the rug the incompatibilities of evolution and religion." Provine insists that evolution finds no intelligent design operating in nature and "no such thing as immortality or life after death." In fact, according to Provine, "we're produced by a process that gives not one damn about us."

Peter Steinfels, the *New York Times* religion reporter, heard Provine speak at a symposium on the *Scopes* Trial held at Vanderbilt University in 1995 and concluded: "It is easy to look back at the battle between rural piety and city cynicism waged seventy years ago in the Dayton courthouse, and feel superior. But maybe those people were right in thinking that something very important was at stake." The man who has been made a laughing stock thanks in part to *Inherit the Wind* seems actually to have understood all this in 1925. "The evolutionists have not been honest with the public," declared Bryan (who was, for what it's worth, a member of the American Academy for the Advancement of Science). He cautioned that "Christians who have allowed themselves to be deceived into believing that evolution is a beneficent, or even a rational, process have been associating with those who either do not understand its implications or dare not avow their knowledge of these implications." In *Inherit the Wind*, Drummond gives a tough-sounding speech about the tradeoffs of progress, instructing the jury that every advance of civilization requires that something be surrendered: "Darwin moved us forward to a hilltop, where we could look back and see the way from which we came. But for this view, this insight, this knowledge, we must abandon our faith in the pleasant poetry of Genesis." Yet, by play's end, Drummond is purveying some pleasant poetry of his own, indicating that Darwin and the Bible are compatible for all but a few religious fanatics.

Evolution's Unanswered Questions

Even the certainty of the doctrine of evolution was considerably oversimplified in both the real *Scopes* Trial and the fictional version in *Inherit the Wind*. Professor Metcalf testified at the real trial, "It is impossible for a normal human being, cognizant of the facts, to have the slightest doubt about the fact of evolution," and the fictional Drummond argues, "What Bertram Cates spoke quietly one spring afternoon in the Hillsboro High School is . . . [as] incontrovertible as geometry in every enlightened community of minds."

But is it? Bryan shrewdly described evolution as a hypothesis—"millions of guesses strung together"—rather than proven theory. And he knew what was missing: "There is not a scientist in all the world who can trace one single species to any other." Nearly a century and a half after the publication of *On the Origin of Species*, the proof for Darwin's theory remains spotty, according to Phillip E. Johnson and others. Bryan sounds at least reasonable when he argues, "If the results of evolution were unimportant, one might require less proof in support of the hypothesis, but before accepting a new philosophy of life, built upon a materialistic foundation, we have reason to demand something more than guesses."

Freedom of Thought or Reverse Bigotry?

Ultimately, however, the truth of evolution is not the theme of *Inherit the Wind*, but the "right to think," and even the "right to be wrong." (The film adds a "right to be lonely" for the misanthropic Hornbeck.) What the play seeks ultimately to defend are the larger prerogatives of "the broad, liberal, critical, cynical, skeptical, and tolerant mind." After the trial, Cates' fiancee Rachel, who has left her father's joylessly pious household, recites the lesson she has learned as she joins the forces of the enlightened:

> You see, I haven't really thought very much. I was always afraid of what I might think—so it seemed safer not to think at all. But now I know. A thought is like a child inside our body. It has to be born. . . . Bad or good, it doesn't make any difference. The ideas have to come out—like children.

Of course, such a simple choice between bigotry and enlightenment is central to the contemporary liberal vision of which *Inherit the Wind* is a typical expression. But while it stands nominally for tolerance, latitude, and freedom of thought, the play is full of the self-righteous certainty that it deplores in the fundamentalist camp. Some critics have detected the play's sanctimonious tone—"bigotry in reverse," as Andrew Sarris called it—even while appreciating its dramatic quality and well-written leading roles. The play reveals a great deal about a mentality that demands open-mindedness and excoriates dogmatism, only to advance its own certainties more insistently—that promotes tolerance and intellectual integrity but stoops to vilifying the opposition, falsifying reality, and distorting history in the service of its agenda.

In fact, a more historically accurate dramatization of the *Scopes* Trial than *Inherit the Wind* might have been far richer and more interesting—and might also have given its audiences a genuine dramatic tragedy to watch. It would not have sent its audience home full of moral superiority and happy thoughts about the march of progress. The truth is not that Bryan was wrong about the dangers of the philosophical materialism that Darwinism presupposes but that he was right, not that he was a once great man disfigured by fear of the future but that he was one of the few to see where a future devoid of the transcendent would lead. The antievolutionist crusade to control what is taught in the schools may not have been the answer, and Bryan's own approach may have been too narrow. But the real tragedy lies in the losing fight that he and others like him waged against a modernity increasingly deprived of spiritual foundations.

The First Amendment and Freedom of Speech in the *Scopes* Trial and *Inherit the Wind*

David Depew

David Depew is a professor in the Department of Communication Studies at the University of Iowa and author of Darwinism Evolving: Systems Dynamics and the Genealogy of Natural Selection.

In the following essay, Depew argues that while Inherit the Wind *is a play about freedom of speech, the* Scopes *trial, which inspired the play, was not. Instead, the trial was, specifically, a defense of the First Amendment's establishment clause, which prohibits the government from favoring any religion or sect. So while the theme of religious freedom was prevalent in both the play and the trial, the trial was a legal issue, not one of personal conviction as the play depicts it.*

To demand that a novel, play, or film that refers to historical events conform strictly to the facts is to misunderstand art. It is even more churlish to complain that something has been left out. Nonetheless, if you use *ITW* [*Inherit the Wind*] to teach history, government, religion, biology, or even literature, I think you should compare the trial as portrayed in the play and the 1960 film based on it with the real thing, perhaps asking your students to do some research and report back. The gap between the fictional account and its original, that is to say, might be a good topic for classroom inquiry.

David Depew, "Inherit the Wind Versus the Scopes Trial: The Play as a Teaching Tool," *Inheriting Inherit the Wind: Debating the Play as a Teaching Tool*, vol. 1, April 2008, pp. 151–57. Copyright © Springer Science + Business Media, LLC 2008. Reproduced by permission of the publisher, conveyed through Copyright Clearance Center, Inc., and the author.

The play or the film can be a useful and accurate pedagogical tool, but I think good teaching and learning will happen only if *ITW* comes with a few "liner notes," some of which I now offer.

An Assault on the First Amendment

The Preface to the play asks audiences to experience the plot not as history but as a cautionary fable in which ignorance and superstition are morally, if not legally, bested by the spirit of free inquiry and free expression. Did the authors seriously think that the audience would not recognize this as the *Scopes* trial? Of course not. In the Preface they acknowledge that "the events that took place in Dayton, Tennessee . . . in 1925 are clearly the genesis of the play." In spite of the fact that [authors Jerome] Lawrence and [Robert E.] Lee go on to disclaim any intent to be accurate or historical at all, however, audiences—even those who read the Preface—do regularly take *ITW* to be about the *Scopes* trial. In fact, the play and the 1960 film (which has no preface) have fixed most people's image of that event as firmly as [Charles] Dickens's *A Tale of Two Cities* has forever fixed our highly inaccurate image of the French Revolution. If you show the film or have students read the play in a biology or history class, where facts are the currency, this impression is likely to be intensified. Hillsboro *is* Dayton. Matthew Brady *is* William Jennings Bryan. Henry Drummond *is* Clarence Darrow. Hornbeck *is* the famous reporter H.L. Mencken.

Why, then, did Lawrence and Lee instruct the audience not to do what the play encourages them to do? The answer, I think, is that, by recasting history as myth, they were encouraging their audience to blur Scopes with [Renaissance Italian physicist, mathematician, astronomer, and philosopher] Galileo and the Salem witches, whose trials Arthur Miller had used as a vehicle for attacking McCarthyism [a policy of finding and rooting out American Communists in the 1950s, led by Senator Joseph McCarthy] in his 1953 play *The Crucible* and, more recently, with [Nicola] Sacco and [Bartolomeo] Vanzetti [whose 1927 conviction and execution were controversial because of the question of a fair trial], whose fates as American leftists had been dramatized in Maxwell Anderson's *Winterset*, which served Lawrence and Lee as a model. The Preface warns that what took place in Dayton "not too long ago . . . could happen tomorrow." People who attend the contemporary Broadway revival of *ITW* will undoubtedly see Lawrence and Lee as presciently predicting the rise of the latter-day religious right's reiterated crusade to blunt the teaching of evolution. However, they were doing no such thing. They had McCarthy's assault on first amendment freedoms on the brain.

The Play vs. the True Trial

The stage directions portray Hillsboro as a "sleepy obscure country town about to be awakened." That helps set a mythic mood. However, Dayton was no such place. It was a new, if small, commercial center whose leading citizens provoked the trial to create a profitable media circus. Nor was its religious sensibility that of Hillsboro's Reverend Jeremiah Brown, whose speeches are indeed "Jeremiads" [doom-saying tirades] and whose obsession with fiery damnation sounds like [New England Puritan minister connected with the Salem witch trials of 1692–93] Cotton Mather. Truth be told, Dayton was in the throes of a very new-fangled version of the old time religion. In contravention of the traditional Protestant call to interpret Scripture for oneself, the Fundamentalist movement, which had been instigated as recently as 1910, demanded literalism to push back so-called "modernist" or "liberal" forms of biblical interpretation, which it took to be corrupting the mainline churches. Evolution got into the act because it required a non-literal interpretation of *Genesis*. A good deal of the North-South tension alluded to in the play was about this issue. In the early twentieth century, American Protestantism, the deepest stratum of our cultural life, was breaking into two camps, creating a white-white cultural and political divide that persists to this day. The Liberal Protestant churches of the North were liberal because they had a liberal, or interpretively free, approach to Scripture, not because they were full of liberals as we now understand the term. That allowed them to think that evolution and *Genesis* are compatible. Fundamentalists denied this. They thought liberalism about Scriptures would lead to liberalism about morality. Their contemporary avatars think that is just what happened.

The play vaguely casts the issue in the trial as freedom of inquiry and speech. It has Bert Cates suffer imprisonment for using his mind. But [John] Scopes was never put in jail, and the fledgling American Civil Liberties Union (ACLU) did not challenge the right of school boards, local communities, or states to compel teachers to stick to the approved curriculum, as they still do not. In fact, teaching the approved curriculum is exactly what Scopes did. He got the text from which he taught, Hunter's *Civic Biology*—a eugenicist [an adherent of eugenics, or a belief in human species improvement through natural selection] tract urging students to watch carefully who they kiss or marry; that is the "civic" part—from the approved textbook depository. The trial was about the first amendment, all right, but it was not about freedom of inquiry or speech. It was about the establishment clause, which forbids states and the federal government to favor any particular religion or sect. The ACLU's argument was that Tennessee was violating this clause by sanctioning one, and only one, interpretation of the Bible. The defense also argued that you could not responsibly teach biology, as the state constitution required, unless you at least mentioned evolution.

This case was argued most fully by the natty divorced Catholic lawyer Dudley Field Malone, who has no counterpart in *ITW*. In his summation, Malone said that the Bible should be kept "in the world of your individual judgment, in the world of the Protestant conscience that I heard so much about when I was a boy." He also said that nothing about evolution logically precluded religious belief. Therefore, Scopes could not possibly have violated the law against teaching anything inconsistent with the Bible. The speech was greeted with such enthusiastic applause that, according to Mencken, Darrow turned to him and said, "Good God! That scoundrel will hang the jury." An acquittal would have defeated the defense's purpose, which was to get Scopes convicted, but in a way that would lay the groundwork for a law-testing appeal. This strategy was upended when Judge Raulston ruled out the oral testimony of all but one of defense's expert witnesses, seven biologists and geologists who saw no inherent contradiction between evolution and the means by which God went about the work of creation (the judge did allow their statements to be included in the transcript). In doing so, Raulston was upholding the prosecution's contention that all this stuff was irrelevant to the narrow issue of whether Scopes had actually violated the law. *ITW* preserves this moment, but lacking its legal context, ascribes the judge's reason for refusing to hear the witnesses to an Orwellian Catch-22 [a socially unjust paradox, characterized by author George Orwell], according to which the law against teaching evolution itself precluded letting witnesses who denied the logical inconsistency of evolution and the Bible on the stand. More bigoted and perverse constraints on freedom of speech.

Populist Literalism

That seemed to end the matter, with the crestfallen Mencken regretting that the anticipated Darrow-Bryan confrontation he had been touting to his readers like a prize fight would not take place. Then, the defense decided to make its point by picking up the other end of the stick: expertise on the meaning of the Bible. Cunningly, Darrow goaded Bryan into testifying as an expert on this subject. Big mistake. Darrow cleverly squeezed Bryan between literalist fundamentalism and his own quasi-modernist interpretation of *Genesis*, according to which, biblical days could mean entire geological eras. The admission was stunning not because Bryan confounded the local yokels, but because he was supporting the defense's main contention!

This moment is badly misrepresented in *ITW* and the film. Brady shows his fundamentalist credentials by asserting [seventeenth-century Irish] Bishop [James] Usher's chronology. "The Lord began the Creation on the 23rd of October in the Year 4004 B.C. at 9:00 A.M.," he says. Asked by Drummond whether the 7 days each had 24 hours, Brady says he does not know. "What do you think?" asks Drummond. "I don't think about things like that," says Brady. He does not think. He does not inquire. He does not use his mind.

In fact, however, even at the end of his life, Bryan was not the vainglorious, close-minded glutton that *ITW* kicks around. If anything, he thought too much with too little equipment for doing so. Like all Populists and Progressives, including Darrow and Mencken, Bryan had opposed the dog-eat-dog Social Darwinism that at the turn of the century served capitalists as a convenient ideology. In the years leading to Dayton, Bryan became even more incensed by the eugenics movement, which he saw, not entirely unreasonably, as the latest incarnation of Darwinism. He also knew that eugenics was being pawned off by self-styled Progressive elites onto high school teachers in texts like Hunter's *Civic Biology*. Reasons for thinking that a truly scientific Darwinism not corrupted by either Social Darwinism or eugenics still lay in the future. However, Bryan was long gone by the time the Modern Evolutionary Synthesis arrived on the scene. Therefore, for him, the only way back toward community-based populist self-government was to oppose Darwinism in all its forms and to move ever more logically, fatally, and tragically toward biblical literalism.

Drummond as a Hero of Free Speech

Drummond is an uncomplicated liberal who defends free inquiry in every possible venue. One can readily see him sticking up for [James] Joyce's *Ulysses* or [D.H.] Lawrence's *Lady Chatterly's Lover* [both of which caused controversy over their material, which was considered obscene in their times]. He walks off the stage with both the Bible and [evolutionary theorist Charles Darwin's] *Origin of Species* in his briefcase. Harking back to [French Enlightenment philosopher] Voltaire, he defends Brady's right to be wrong against the cynicism of Hornbeck, who in turn reproaches him for being an atheist who believes in God. However, Clarence Darrow was nothing like this. He opposed what he called "the eugenics cult" not for Bryan's reasons, but because he was an environmental, not a genetic, determinist. He was in the tradition of naturalistic, muckraking novelists like Theodore Dreiser and Frank Norris. Darrow did not think that the teenage murderers [Nathan] Leopold and [Richard] Loeb, whom he had just successfully saved from the death penalty, were victims of their ancestors' bad seed, but of their own background and their unfortunate habit of reading [nineteenth-century German philosopher Friedrich] Nietzsche and [nineteenth-century Russian novelist Fyodor] Dostoyevsky. In developing his arguments against capital punishment, which was his stock in trade, Darrow pinned his hopes on empowering a class of social scientific experts. What enraged him about his former political ally Bryan, and provoked him to show him up, was that, in his view, Bryan had led the American left into a right-wing, know-nothing dead end.

Lawrence and Lee put into Hornbeck's mouth Darrow's self-exculpating remark that Bryan had "died of a busted belly." This change from the historical record allows Drummond to be the hero of free speech and inquiry that the play wants him to be. He reproaches Hornbeck for talking in this disrespectful way because, he says, Brady had once been a great man. He spoke his mind. He exercised his right to be wrong. Darrow made the remark, however, not only because he was unrepentant, but because he was a materialist, whose environmental determinism resisted all ideal or spiritual explanations. In his view, Bryan really did die of a busted belly. Nor, for that matter, was Mencken a cynical, materialistic bystander like Hornbeck. He was a passionate skeptic who opposed in equal measure both sides of the growing schism in American Protestantism and, relatedly, the Democratic Party. He rallied against the ungrounded scientism of the Progressive elites, especially eugenics, as well as the superstitious tribalism of what he was the first to call "the Bible belt."

Fundamentalism vs. Modernism

In his best-selling, Pulitzer prize–winning account of the *Scopes* trial, *Summer for the Gods*, Edward Larson shows that, in framing their play, Lawrence and Lee passed on "the Scopes legend" that has remained constant ever since Frederick Lewis Allen's (1931) description of the trial in his journalistic portrait of the 1920s, *Only Yesterday*. The "not too long ago" of Lawrence and Lee's Preface echoes Allen's title as well as his mythic sense of time. Allen redescribes the trial as a titanic conflict between the freedom of inquiry on which science depends and religious belief generally, not just fundamentalism. Noticing that this is not exactly how the trial was framed or received at the time, Allen writes, "The issue of the Scopes trial as the great mass of newspaper readers saw it was nothing so abstruse as the rights of taxpayers versus academic freedom. In the eyes of the public the trial was a battle between fundamentalism and twentieth century skepticism (assisted by modernism)." However, nothing as abstruse as academic freedom was, in fact, at issue in the *Scopes* trial. Fundamentalism versus modernism is not only what readers thought the trial was about. That is what it *was* about. It is no doubt true that the expansion and protection of personal rights and freedoms that defines the political liberalism despised by contemporary fundamentalists was already a gleam in the eye of the ACLU. It is also true that the rudiments of this tolerant philosophy were soon to be incubated by the New Deal [President Franklin Roosevelt's economic programs designed to raise America up from the Great Depression] (partly as a way of easing tensions between the Northern and Southern halves of the Democratic Party). However, these themes, which stand out in *ITW*, are barely visible in the transcript of the *Scopes* trial.

By using *ITW* as a stimulus for research, reports, and classroom debates, I think students can learn to engage in responsible citizenly discussions about how science, religion, and society are properly related in and through our contentious democratic forms of public discourse. I cannot imagine, however, that such exercises will bear much fruit if they do not focus on the gap between the actual trial and *ITW* in its several context-dependent incarnations. Students cannot get started or go very far in this direction without some background and some guidance.

Freedom of Thought Should Be for All

Phillip E. Johnson

Phillip E. Johnson is Jefferson E. Peyser Professor of Law, Emeritus, at the University of California–Berkeley School of Law and is considered the father of the intelligent design movement, which rejects the theory of evolution as fact.

Johnson believes that all individuals, not merely those in power, should be granted freedom of speech. In the following selection, Johnson compares Inherit the Wind's *antievolutionists with current-day antireligious individuals. In Johnson's mind,* Inherit the Wind, *and the publicity it generated, sparked antireligious fervor that equaled the antievolution fervor the play condemned. Should not all individuals be allowed freedom of speech? asks Johnson.*

After almost every lecture I give, some person—usually a parent—asks me for advice about how to come across as a reasonable person when speaking up at a school board meeting against the dogmatic teaching of Darwinian evolution [the theory of naturalist Charles Darwin]. People who only want unbiased, honest science education that sticks to the evidence are bewildered by the reception they get when they try to make their case. Their specific points are brushed aside, and they are dismissed out of hand as religious fanatics. The newspapers report that "creationists" are once again trying to censor science education because it offends their religious beliefs. Why is it so hard for reasoned criticism of biased teaching to get a hearing?

The answer to that question begins with a play called *Inherit the Wind*, which was made into a movie in 1960 starring

Spencer Tracy, Gene Kelly, and Frederic March. You can rent the movie at any movie store with a "classics" section, and I urge you to do so and watch it carefully after reading this [selection]. The play is a fictionalized treatment of the "Scopes Trial" of 1925, the legendary courtroom confrontation in Tennessee over the teaching of evolution. *Inherit the Wind* is a masterpiece of propaganda, which promotes a stereotype of the public debate about creation and evolution that gives all virtue and intelligence to the Darwinists. The play did not create the stereotype, but it presented it in the form of a powerful story that sticks in the minds of journalists, scientists, and intellectuals generally.

If you speak out about the teaching of evolution in a public hearing, the audience and the reporters will be placing your words in the context of *Inherit the Wind*. Whether you know it or not, you are playing a role in a play. The question is, which role in the story will be yours? . . .

Modernist Understanding of Freedom

[Although there are discrepancies between the play and history,] the play has had so much impact that its story is more important than what really happened. The play is not primarily about a single event; it is about the modernist understanding of freedom. Once upon a time, the story says, the world was ruled by cruel religious oppressors called Christians, similar to the wicked stepmother and stepsisters in Cinderella, who tried to prevent people from thinking and from marrying their true love. Liberation from this oppression came via Darwin, who taught us that our real Creator was a natural process which leaves human reason free to make up new rules whenever we want. Most modernist intellectuals interpret the story that way, and of course a liberated Cinderella is not likely to give the wicked stepmother another chance to enslave her. Whatever she says, Cinderella knows who she is and what she wants to do.

Read that way, *Inherit the Wind* is a bitter attack upon Christianity, or at least the conservative Christianity that considers the Bible to be in some sense a reliable historical record. The rationalists have all the good lines, and all the virtues. [Prosecutor Matthew Harrison] Brady and [Reverend Jeremiah] Brown are a combination of folly, pride, and malice, and their followers are so many mindless puppets. One would suppose from the play that Christianity has no program other than to teach hatred. At the surface level the play is a smear, although it is one which smears an acceptable target and hence is considered suitable for use in the public schools.

Just how ugly the smear is came home to me the first time I saw the movie, in a theater next to Harvard University (at a time when I would have called myself an agnostic). The demonstrative student audience freely jeered at the rubes of Hillsboro, whooped with delight at every wisecrack from [journalist E.K.] Hornbeck or [defense lawyer Henry] Drummond, and revelled in Brady's humiliation. It occurred to me that the Harvard students were reacting much like the worst of the Hillsboro citizens in the movie. They thought they were showing how smart they were by aping the prejudices of their teachers, and by being cruel to the ghost of William Jennings Bryan—who was probably a much better man than any of them. Maybe Hillsboro isn't just Dayton, Tennessee. Maybe sometimes it's Harvard, or Berkeley.

The Story Told Another Way

That memory has stayed with me, and shows that there may be more than one way to interpret the play. . . . [L]et me retell the story at a different level, with just a tad of artistic license.

A brilliant young teacher develops a following because he has exciting ideas that open up a new way of life. His friends and students love him, but the ruling elders of his community hate the very thought of him. These elders are themselves cruel hypocrites, who pile up burdens on the people and do not lift a finger to help them. The elders rule the people by fear, and are themselves ruled by fear. They substitute dogmas and empty rituals for the true teaching they once knew, which commands truth and love as its first principles.

The elders want to destroy the teacher who threatens their control over the people, but his behavior and character are so exemplary that they can find no fault to justify condemning him. They plan to entrap him by convincing one of his closest friends to betray him. Eventually they are able to arrange a rigged legal proceeding and get a guilty verdict. Their victory is empty, however. The teacher wins even when he apparently loses, and he sums up his teaching in these words: "You shall know the truth, and the truth shall make you free."

Does that story sound familiar? Of course Bert Cates is not Jesus, although the play does portray him as virtually sinless. It would be more accurate to say that the authors aimed to give Cates and Drummond the virtues of Cinderella and [ancient Greek philosopher] Socrates. My point is that even this most seemingly anti-Biblical of dramas achieves its moral effect by borrowing elements from the gospel, which is the good news of how we can be delivered from the power of sin. Sin has its power over us in many ways, and one of them is through the mind control practiced by fearful and hypocritical religious authorities. The independent mind that overthrows such oppressive power is good news for everyone but the oppressor.

Inherit the Wind is therefore probably truer than its authors knew. There is nothing wrong with its basic story of liberation. That story itself becomes a vehicle of oppression, however, when it invites the people with power to cast themselves as the liberators. It's like the dictators of the former Soviet Union calling themselves the champions of the poor working man. Whatever may have been the case a long time ago, by the time the movie was made Bert Cates and Henry Drummond were the ones with the power to shut other people up. . . .

A Reversal of Power

When Henry Drummond was humiliating Matthew Harrison Brady on the witness stand, he accused Brady of setting himself up as God, by presuming to suppress freedom of thought in others. Drummond warned Brady that some day the power might be in other hands, saying "Suppose Mr. Cates had enough influence and lung power to railroad through the State Legislature a law that only *Darwin* should be taught in the schools!"

That possibility may have seemed remote in Hillsboro, but of course it is exactly what happened later. The real story of the *Scopes* trial is that the stereotype it promoted helped the Darwinists to capture the power of the law, and they have since used the law to prevent other people from thinking independently. By labelling any fundamental dissent from Darwinism as "religion," they are able to ban criticism of the official evolution story from public education far more effectively than the teaching of evolution was banned from the Tennessee schools in the 1920s. But how has this reversal been accomplished in a voting democracy? Given that a majority of Americans still believe that God is our creator, how have the Darwinists been able to obtain so much influence and lung power?

The play answers that question too. In the final scene of *Inherit the Wind*, when the jury returns to the courtroom to deliver its verdict, a character identified as "Radio Man" appears in the courtroom, carrying a large microphone. He explains to the judge that the microphone is connected by direct wire to station WGN in Chicago. Radio Man proceeds to report directly to the public on the proceedings as they happen. Brady, famed for decades as an orator with a huge voice, attempts to speak into the microphone but can't master the technique. During Brady's final tirade the radio program director decides that his speech has become boring, and Radio Man breaks in to announce that the station will return to the

Chicago studio for some music. The stage directions describe this as Brady's "final indignity," and it brings on his fatal stroke.

One-Sided Freedom of Speech

The microphone (i.e., the news media) can nullify Brady's power by (in effect) out-shouting him. But does this development imply liberation, or a new form of control that will be more oppressive than the old one? There is only one microphone in that courtroom, and whoever decides when to turn it on or off controls what the world will learn about the trial. That is why what happened in the real-life *Scopes* trial hardly matters; the writers and producers of *Inherit the Wind* owned the microphone, making their interpretation far more important than the reality. Bert Cates didn't have enough lung power to make law in Dayton, but his successors had enough microphone power to take over the law at the national level.

When the creation/evolution conflict is replayed in our own media-dominated times, the microphone owners of the media get to decide who plays the heroes, and who plays the villains. What this has meant for decades is that Darwinists—who are now the legal and political power holders—nonetheless appear before the microphone as Bert Cates or Henry Drummond. The defenders of creation are assigned the role of Brady, or of the despicable Reverend Brown. No matter what happens in the real courtroom, or the real school room, the microphones keep telling the same old story.

This has very practical consequences. I have found it practically impossible, for example, to get newspapers to acknowledge that there are scientific problems with Darwinism that are quite independent of what anybody thinks about the Bible. The reporters may seem to get the point during an interview, but after the story goes through the editors it almost always comes back with the same formula: creationists are trying to substitute Genesis for the science textbook. Scientific journals follow the same practice. That Matthew Harrison Brady might have valid scientific points to make just isn't in the script.

Inherit the Wind Applies Today

Occasionally a dissenter from Darwinism threatens to take over the role of Bert Cates. Here is one example: Danny Phillips was a 15-year-old high school junior in the Denver area, who thinks for himself. His class was assigned to watch a NOVA program produced with government funds for National Public Television, which stated the usual evolutionary story as fact. Its story went something like this: "The first organized form of primitive life was a tiny protozoan. . . . From these one-celled organisms evolved all life on earth."

Science education today encourages students to memorize that sort of naturalistic doctrine and repeat it on a test as fact. Because Danny has a special interest in truth, however, and because his father is pastor of a church that has an interest in questioning evolutionary naturalism, Danny knew that this claim of molecule to man evolution goes far beyond the scientific evidence. So he wrote a lengthy paper criticizing the NOVA program as propaganda. The school administrators at first agreed that Danny had a point, and tentatively decided to withdraw the NOVA program from the curriculum. That set off a media firestorm.

Of course Danny was making a reasonable point. The doctrine that some known process of evolution turned a protozoan into a human is a philosophical assumption, not something that can be confirmed by experiment or by historical studies of the fossil record. But the fact that administrators seriously considered any dissent from evolutionary naturalism infuriated the Darwinists, who flooded the city's newspapers with their letters. Some of the letters were so venomous that the editorial page editor of the *Denver Post* admitted that her liberal faith had been shaken. She wrote that "these defenders of intellectual freedom behaved, in fact, just like a bunch of conservative Christians. Their's was a different kind of fundamentalism, but no less dogmatic and no less intolerant."

In other words, at least one editor wasn't sure who was playing what role in the revival of *Inherit the Wind*. When his story appeared on CBS television a little later, however, an experienced Darwinist debater named Eugenie Scott was careful to cast Danny as the opponent of learning. She argued that "If Danny Phillips doesn't want to learn evolution, ... that's his own business. But his views should not prevail for 80,000 students who need to learn evolution to be educated." When evolution is the subject, questioning whether the official story is true is enough to make you an enemy of education.

This manufactured image of a high school sophomore censoring science education replaced the real Danny Phillips on national television, just as *Inherit the Wind* replaced the real *Scopes* trial. What Danny said when he got a chance to speak for himself was reported only in a local paper. He said that "Students' minds are to be kept open and not limited by a set of beliefs." That is exactly the right line to take, and Danny had for a moment a partial success in getting past the microphone owners. The CBS network and the Denver school board decided against Danny in the end—but then, the Hillsboro jury also decided against Bert Cates. All they inherited was the wind.

Before *Inherit the Wind,* *Scopes* Put the Law on Trial

Steve Benen

Steve Benen is a contributing writer to The Washington Monthly. *He has written for various publications and has appeared on a number of radio and television news programs, including National Public Radio's* Talk of the Nation.

In the following article, Benen distinguishes between the Scopes *trial and the play and movie* Inherit the Wind. *According to Benen, while the play and movie dramatized many of the events of the trial, some of the events were accurately represented. Most importantly, the character Henry Drummond's courtroom strategy of questioning the antievolution law that, he believed, conflicted with separation of church and state accurately portrayed the real defense lawyer Clarence Darrow's courtroom strategy. Also, the dramatized battle of the minds between Drummond and Matthew Harrison Brady, on the sides of scientific knowledge versus the Bible, respectively, did truly occur between Darrow and prosecutor William Jennings Bryan.*

In one of the first scenes of the 1960 movie *Inherit the Wind,* Bertram Cates, a character based on John T. Scopes, explains to his fiancee from a county jail why he must teach his students evolution and why he refuses to back down. "Tell them they can let my body out of jail if I lock up my mind?" Cates asks. "Could you stand that?"

It Never Happened

His impassioned plea for understanding gives the audience a clear awareness of the struggle the real Scopes was forced to endure. There's only one problem with the scene: It never happened.

Steve Benen, "Inherit the Myth?" *Church & State*, vol. 53, July 2000, pp. 15–17. Copyright © 2000 Americans United for Separation of Church and State. Reproduced by permission.

Scopes issued no plea for empathy, there was no fiancee and the real Scopes was never arrested. In fact, [the award-winning play and] the popular film that was nominated for four Academy Awards and helped shape the American understanding of the "Scopes Monkey Trial" for decades is an inadequate reflection of history.

In Hollywood's version of the case, dialogue was created, locations of events were altered, the names of people and places were changed and some characters were invented while actual participants disappeared.

Regardless, the real story of the *Scopes* trial needed little exaggeration as a dramatic episode in American history. The events that unfolded over 11 days in mid-July 1925 were spectacular enough to earn their status as the "Trial of the Century."

In his Pulitzer Prize–winning book, *Summer for the Gods*, Edward J. Larson details the accurate account of the famous trial.

The story started in January, when the Tennessee legislature passed a law prohibiting the teaching of "any theory that denies the story of the Divine Creation of man as taught in the Bible." Immediately after it was signed into law, the American Civil Liberties Union offered legal representation to any teacher charged under the statute.

At the time, Dayton, Tenn., was a small town with a struggling economy and a population that had dwindled to 1,800. George W. Rappleyea, who managed mines in the area, saw mention of the ACLU's offer in a local newspaper and determined that what Dayton needed was some publicity. With all of the national attention surrounding the legislature's passage of an anti-evolution bill, he figured a trial ought to generate at least as much interest.

Rappleyea met with local school officials and convinced them of the benefits that a trial could generate. He and his friends then asked Scopes if he'd mind doing them a favor.

In a U.K. production of Inherit the Wind, *Kevin Spacey dramatizes the role of Henry Drummond (based on defense lawyer Clarence Darrow) and his aggressive strategy of questioning the antievolution law.* © Robbie Jack/Corbis.

The film version of the *Scopes* trial shows the young teacher in class, explaining natural selection to a classroom of interested teenagers. County prosecutors and the local minister stand in the back of the room and when Scopes begins to discuss Charles Darwin, he is promptly taken into custody.

A Trial for Media Attention

The truth was less exciting. Scopes told Rappleyea he wasn't sure if he ever actually taught the chapter on biological evolution. (The 24-year-old teacher later had to prompt his students on what to say in order to secure his own indictment.) Nevertheless, he acknowledged that he taught from the science text and agreed to allow himself to be used for a challenge to Tennessee's new law. The same meeting saw a local justice of the peace issue a warrant and Scopes get charged. Scopes, instead of going to jail, went to play tennis. With that, one of the most successful publicity stunts of the 20th century was set in motion.

The trial itself generated an incredible amount of media attention in large part because of the prominent lawyers on each side. For the prosecution, William Jennings Bryan, a celebrated religious leader and the Democratic nominee for President in 1896 and 1900, volunteered to take up the cause. For the defense, Clarence Darrow, at the time the most well known defense attorney in the nation, enlisted.

The trial was played out in what Scopes would later describe as "man-killing" heat. Mid-July in Tennessee routinely saw 100-degree days that summer, and the courthouse did not have working air-conditioning. As the [play and] movie accurately portrayed, Judge John T. Raulston allowed the attorneys to ignore traditional attire and appear in court sans [without] jacket and tie.

Putting the Law on Trial

Darrow's courtroom strategy was clear, and even the movie represented it accurately. The character portraying Bryan at one point argues, "It's obvious what he's trying to do. He's trying to make us forget the lawbreaker and put the law on trial!"

Though fictitious dialogue, the point was true. Early on, Darrow even sought to quash the indictment on the grounds that the anti-evolution law was in conflict with the separation of church and state.

"'All men have a natural and indefeasible right to worship Almighty God according to the dictates of their own conscience, and that no preference shall be given by law to any religious establishment or mode of worship,'" Darrow said, reading from the Tennessee Constitution. "Does it? Could you get any more preference, your honor, by law? . . . [The state law] makes the Bible the yard stick to measure every man's intellect, to measure every man's intelligence and to measure every man's learning."

Raulston rejected Darrow's effort against the indictment. It was one of a long series of defeats for Darrow.

In contrast, the prosecution laid out a very simple case: state law forbade teaching evolution, Scopes admitted to teaching evolution, so Scopes was guilty of breaking the law. The prosecution rested a mere half-hour after its opening statement.

Darrow's defense was more complicated. He sought to prove that the law was unconstitutional. Moreover, because many religious leaders from a variety of backgrounds agreed that evolution does not have to conflict with the Bible, Darrow argued that Scopes did not technically violate the law.

Darrow, however, was given little opportunity to mount a defense. Raulston ruled that Darrow's expert witnesses were irrelevant as to Scopes' guilt. They could offer written statements for the record, but the jury would not hear from them.

The War of Words

At this point, the trial seemed over to almost everyone. Several reporters, disappointed by what they saw as an anticlimactic end, left Dayton. What they missed became the confrontation that propelled the trial into the history books.

The judge moved the proceedings from the courtroom to the courthouse lawn for what most assumed would be the end of the trial. Instead Darrow called an expert witness to testify about the source of scientific knowledge mandated by state law, the Bible. His witness was William Jennings Bryan.

A reported 3,000 people turned out for the war of words between the two legends. While the [play's and] movie's version of the testimony was exaggerated, Darrow did question Bryan relentlessly on his literal interpretation of Scripture, asking him to explain what Darrow saw as biblical inconsistencies and oddities such as the existence of Cain's wife, Jonah's three-day visit inside a whale and Joshua's stopping of the sun.

Press accounts were nearly unanimous in declaring Darrow the winner of the rhetorical heavyweight fight. Darrow wrote a note to Baltimore journalist H.L. Mencken, who earned national attention for his coverage of the trial, in which the attorney said, "I made up my mind to show the country what an ignoramus he was and I succeeded."

Case Settled, but Far from Over

But for Darrow, even this victory was short lived. The judge ended his examination of Bryan and expunged Bryan's remarks from the record, ruling that his testimony could "shed no light" on the matter at hand.

The defense had no choice but to surrender. An exasperated Darrow, eager to move forward with an appeal, asked the jurors to find Scopes guilty. After nine minutes of deliberation, they did.

In what seemed then to be a trivial matter, after the verdict was read, the judge imposed a $100 fine on Scopes, despite a state law allowing the jury to decide the amount. When *Tennessee v. Scopes* ultimately reached the state Supreme Court, the teacher's conviction was overturned because of this procedural error. The court, however, upheld the state's anti-evolution law.

The *Scopes* trial took a heavy toll on Bryan, and he died a short time afterwards. Mencken joked, "God aimed at Darrow, missed, and hit Bryan instead."

The matter was not permanently resolved for almost another half-century, when in 1967, Tennessee repealed the law that censored evolution from state classrooms.

Inherit the Wind Mistakenly Celebrates the End of the Antievolution Movement

Edward J. Larson

Edward J. Larson is a professor and the Hugh & Hazel Darling Chair in Law at Pepperdine University in California. His book Summer for the Gods: The Scopes Trial and America's Continuing Debate over Science and Religion *won the 1998 Pulitzer Prize for History.*

In the following excerpt, Larson discusses how, although Jerome Lawrence and Robert Edwin Lee stressed that Inherit the Wind *was not history, the play left an undeniable impact on the perception of the* Scopes *trial. But while conservatives might oppose the play's unkind representation of the religious side, some evolutionists believe the play has struck them harder. Larson mentions the belief that the play's siding with evolution might have given evolutionists a false sense of security in a climate of creationist resurgence. If the resurgence is successful, society could experience a loss of freedom similar to the repressive McCarthy era the play railed against.*

[T]he] grim fascination with the *Scopes* trial as a foreshadowing of McCarthyism inspired the single most influential retelling of the tale, Jerome Lawrence and Robert E. Lee's play, *Inherit the Wind*. In contrast to [other] comic portrayal[s] of the trial, Lawrence and Lee presented it as present-day drama. "*Inherit the Wind* does not pretend to be journalism," they wrote in their published introduction for the play, "It is not 1925. The stage directions set the time as 'Not too long ago.' It might have been yesterday. It could be tomorrow." In writing this, they did not intend to present antievolutionism as an ongoing danger—to the contrary, they perceived that threat as safely past; rather, their concern was the McCarthy-era [the 1950s years of weeding out suspected Communists in America led by Senator Joseph McCarthy] blacklisting of writers and actors (the play opened on Broadway in 1955). "In the 1950s, Lee and his partner became very concerned with the spread of McCarthyism," a student who interviewed him reported. "Lawrence and Lee felt that McCarthyism paralleled some aspects of the *Scopes* trial. Lee worried, 'I was very concerned when laws were passed, when legislation limits our freedom to speak; silence is a dangerous thing.'" Tony Randall, who starred in the original Broadway cast, later wrote, "Like *The Crucible* [Arthur Miller's 1953 play that dramatized the Salem witch trials of the late seventeenth century], *Inherit the Wind* was a response to and a product of McCarthyism. In each play, the authors looked to American history for a parallel."

Inaccurate History, but Brilliant Theater

For their model, Lawrence and Lee took Maxwell Anderson's *Winterset*, a play loosely based on the Sacco-Vanzetti case [in which Nicola Sacco and Bartolomeo Vanzetti were convicted and executed for murder in 1927 in a controversial and, many say, unfair trial]. Anderson had claimed "a poet's license to expand, develop, and interpolate, dramatize and comment," Lawrence and Lee later explained. "We asked for the same liberty . . . to allow the actuality to be the springboard for the larger drama so that the stage could thunder a meaning that wasn't pinned to a given date or a given place."

The play was not history, as Lawrence and Lee stressed in their introduction. "Only a handful of phrases have been taken from the actual transcript of the famous *Scopes* trial. Some of the characters of the play are related to the colorful figures in that battle of giants; but they have a life and language of their own—and, therefore, names of their own." For their two star-ring roles, the writers chose sound-alike names: [William Jennings] Bryan became Brady and [Clarence] Darrow was Drummond. The role of the Baltimore *Sun's* H.L. Mencken was expanded to become the Baltimore *Herald's* E.K. Hornbeck. [John] Scopes became Cates. Tom Stewart diminished into a minor role as Tom Davenport. [Defense attorneys Dudley] Malone, [Arthur] Hays, [and John] Neal, [businessman George] Rappleyea, and the ACLU [American Civil Liberties Union, which instigated the *Scopes* trial] disappeared from the story altogether, as did the WCFA [World Christian Fundamentals Association, who brought in Bryan] and all the home-town prosecutors. Dayton (called Hillsboro) gained a mayor and a fire-breathing fundamentalist pastor who subjugated townspeople until Darrow came to set them free with his cool reason. Scopes acquired a fiancée—"She is twenty-two, pretty, but not beautiful," the stage directions read, and she is the fearsome preacher's daughter. "They had to invent romance for the balcony set," Scopes later joked. It may not have been accurate history, but it was brilliant theater—and it all but replaced the actual trial in the nation's memory. The play wove three fundamental changes into the story line (in addition to countless minor ones), all of which served the writers' objectives of debunking McCarthyism.

A Fabricated Witch Hunt

The first change involved Scopes and Dayton. Ralph Waldo Emerson once described a mob as "a society of bodies voluntarily bereaving themselves of reason." In *Inherit the Wind*, Cates becomes the innocent victim of a mob-enforced anti-evolution law. The stage directions begin, *"It is important to the concept of the play that the town is always visible, looming there, as much on trial as the individual defendant."* In the movie version, the town fathers haul Cates out of his classroom for teaching evolution. Limited to a few sets, the play begins with the defendant in jail explaining to his fiancée, "You know why I did it. I had the book in my hand, Hunter's

Civic Biology. I opened it up, and read to my sophomore science class Chapter 17, [evolution theorist Charles] Darwin's *Origin of Species*." For innocently doing his job, Cates "is threatened with fine and imprisonment," according to the script. This change provoked trial correspondent Joseph Wood Krutch, "The little town of Dayton behaved on the whole quite well," he wrote in rebuttal. "The atmosphere was so far from being sinister that it suggested a circus day." Yet, he complained, "The authors of *Inherit the Wind* made it chiefly sinister, a witch hunt of the sort we are now all too familiar with." Scopes never truly faced jail, Krutch reminded readers, and the defense actually instigated the trial. "Thus it was all in all a strange sort of witch trial," he concluded, "one in which the accused won a scholarship enabling him to attend graduate school and the only victim was the chief witness for the prosection, poor old Bryan."

Second, the writers transformed Bryan into a mindless, reactionary creature of the mob. Brady was "the biggest man in the country—next to the President, maybe," the audience heard at the outset, who "came here to find himself a stump to shout from. That's all." In the play, he assails evolution solely on narrow biblical grounds (never suggesting the broad social concerns that largely motivated Bryan) and denounces all science as "Godless," rather than the so-called false science of evolution. "*Inherit the Wind* dramatically illustrates why so many Americans continue to believe in the mythical war between science and religion," [science historian] Ronald Numbers later wrote. "But in doing so, it sacrifices the far more complex historical reality."

Brady Debunked, Drummond Uplifted

On the witness stand, Brady responds even more foolishly than Bryan did at the real trial. In *Inherit the Wind*, Brady steadfastly maintains on alleged biblical authority that God created the universe in six twenty-four-hour days beginning "on the 23rd of October in the Year 4004 B.C. at—uh, at 9 A.M.!" The crowd gradually slips away from him as he babbles on, reciting the names of books in the Old Testament. "Mother. They're laughing at me, Mother!" Brady cries to his wife at the close of his testimony. "I can't stand it when they laugh at me!" At a Broadway performance of the play, the constitutional scholar Gerald Gunther became so outraged that, as he later wrote, "for the first time, I walked out of a play in disgust." He explained, "I ended up actually sympathizing with Bryan, even though I was and continue to be opposed to his ideas in the case, simply because the playwrights had drawn the character in such comic strip terms." Even though Bryan in fact opposed including a penalty provision in antievolution laws, the play ends with his character ranting against the small size of the fine imposed by the judge, then fatally collapsing in the courtroom when the now hostile crowd ignores his closing speech. *"The mighty Evolution Law explodes with a pale puff of a wet firecracker,"* the stage directions explain, just as McCarthyism itself died from ridicule.

Just as Lawrence and Lee debunked Brady-Bryan in the eyes of the audience, they uplifted Drummond-Darrow. In *Inherit the Wind*, the Baltimore *Herald* engages the notorious Chicago attorney to defend Cates. Drummond makes his entrance in a *"long, ominous shadow,"* the stage directions instruct, *"hunched over, head forward."* A young girl screams, "It's the Devil!" but he softens as the play proceeds. "All I want is to prevent the clock-stoppers from dumping a load of medieval nonsense in the United States Constitution," he explains at one point; "You've got to stop 'em somewhere."

The Liberal Plea for Tolerance

Drummond remains a self-proclaimed agnostic, but loses his crusading materialism. At the play's end, it is Hornbeck who delivers Darrow's famous line that Bryan "died of a busted belly" and ridicules the Commoner's fool religion. [Bryan was known by the epithet the Great Commoner.] Drummond reacts with anger. "You smart-aleck! You have no more right to spit on his religion than you have a right to spit on my religion! Or lack of it!" he replies. The writers have Drummond issue the liberal's McCarthy-era plea for tolerance that everyone has the "right to be wrong!" The cynical reporter then calls the defense lawyer "more religious" than Brady, and storms off the stage. Left alone in the courtroom, Drummond picks up the defendant's copy of *The Origin of Species* and the judge's Bible. After "*balancing them thoughtfully, as if his hands were scales,*" the stage directions state, the attorney "*jams them in his briefcase, side by side,*" and slowly walks off the now-empty stage. "A bit of religious disinfectant is added to the agnostic legend for audiences whose evolutionary stage is not yet very high," the radical *Village Voice* sneered in its review.

At the time, most published reviews of the stage and screen versions of *Inherit the Wind* criticized the writers' portrayal of the *Scopes* trial. "History has been not increased but almost fatally diminished," the *New Yorker* drama critic complained. "The script wildly and unjustly caricatures the fundamentalists as vicious and narrow-minded hypocrites," the *Time* magazine movie review chided, and "just as wildly and unjustly idealizes their opponents, as personified by Darrow." Reviews appearing in publications ranging from *Commonweal* and the *New York Herald Tribune* to *The New Republic* and the *Village Voice* offered similar critiques.

Inherit the Wind's Durability

Both the play and movie proved remarkably durable, however, despite the critics. After opening at New York's National Theater early in 1955, the stage version played for nearly three years, making it the longest-running drama then on Broadway. A touring cast took the play to major cities around the country during the late fifties. The script gained new life as a screenplay in 1960, resulting in a hit movie starring Spencer

Tracy, Fredric March, and Gene Kelly. John Scopes attended its world premiere in Dayton, and thereafter promoted the movie across the country at the studio's behest. "Of course, it altered the facts of the real trial," Scopes commented, but maintained that "the film captured the emotions in the battle of words between Bryan and Darrow." Sue Hicks [coprosecutor in the *Scopes* trial], the only other major participant to attend the premiere, reacted quite differently to the film. He called it "a travesty on William Jennings Bryan" and nearly purchased television time to denounce it. Since its initial release, the movie has appeared continually on television and video, while the play has become a staple for community and school theatrical groups. By 1967, trial correspondent Joseph Wood Krutch could rightly comment, "Most people who have any notions about the trial get them from the play, *Inherit the Wind*, or from the movie."

All of which bothered Krutch, who had led the liberal media to Dayton. "The play was written more than a generation after the event and its atmosphere is that of the 40's and 50's, not the 20's. This makes for falsification because one of the striking facts about the whole foolish business is just that it was so characteristic of the 20's," he wrote. "That the trial could be a farce, even a farce with sinister aspects, is a tribute to the 20's when, whatever the faults and limitations of that decade, we did not play as rough as we play today." Bryan, for example, offered to pay Scopes's $100 fine; McCarthy, in contrast, destroyed careers and wrecked lives without remorse. Left unchecked, fundamentalist intolerance might have worsened but, given their natures, Bryan and other fundamentalist leaders of the twenties simply were less malign than the McCarthyites. In history classrooms, however, *Inherit the Wind* became a popular instructional tool for teaching students about the twenties. In 1994, for example, the National Center for History in Schools published instructional standards. As a means to educate high school students about changing values during the 1920s, it recommended that teachers "use selections from the *Scopes* trial or excerpts from *Inherit the Wind* to explain how the views of William Jennings Bryan differed from those of Clarence Darrow."

Part of the Folklore of Liberalism

As Krutch noted in 1967, "The events [at Dayton] are more a part of the folklore of liberalism than of history." The astronomer and science popularizer Carl Sagan recognized this when he observed that, even though the *Scopes* trial may have had little lasting impact on American culture, "the movie *Inherit the Wind* probably had a considerable national influence; it was the first time, so far as I know, that American movies made explicit the apparent contradictions and inconsistencies in the book of Genesis." Calvin College scientist Howard J. Van Till, who led the fight against antievolutionism within the evangelical church during the later part of the twentieth century, also stated that "folklore [about the *Scopes* trial] has had a greater impact [on American culture] than the actual historical particulars have had," but he does not so readily concede that *Inherit the Wind* monopolized that folklore. "While many members of the scientific academy might think of the *Scopes* trial as an episode in which Clarence Darrow artfully exposed the ignorant and narrow-minded dogmatism of North American Fundamentalism," he suggested from his experience, "many members of the conservative Christian community might think of it as an episode in which William Jennings Bryan was skillfully manipulated by a skilled but unprincipled lawyer representing an antitheistic scientific establishment."

Ever since *Inherit the Wind* first appeared, conservative Christians have displayed greater interest in countering the popular impression created by it than by the trial. Creation-science leader Henry M. Morris, for example, could attribute the troubles of Bryan at Dayton to his testimony about the age of the earth but, in *Inherit the Wind*, Brady espouses a reading of Genesis every bit as literal as Morris's own. Reflecting on the problems this has caused his movement, Morris discussed a 1973 lecture tour that he gave in New Zealand. "There was a great deal of interest," he complained, "but in city after city, either during my visit or immediately afterward, the government-controlled television channels kept showing the *Scopes* trial motion picture, *Inherit the Wind*, over and over." Advocates of creation-science and critics of Darwinism have repeatedly attempted to explain how *Inherit the Wind* does not fairly represent their position. The trial itself became, as the historian of religion Martin E. Marty later described it, "One final irrelevancy," by which he meant that it gained significance "as an event of media-mythic proportions"—that is, not for what actually occurred, but through its "acquired mythic character." For the general public since 1960, that mythic character largely came through *Inherit the Wind*.

The Light of Reason

The mythic *Scopes* legend remained constant from [the 1920s] through post–World War II history textbooks to *Inherit the Wind*. The Harvard paleontologist Stephen Jay Gould summarized and criticized it as follows: "John Scopes was persecuted, Darrow rose to Scopes's defense and smote the antediluvian ["before the biblical flood"—connoting "ancient"] Bryan, and the antievolution movement then dwindled or ground to at least a temporary halt. All three parts of this story are false." Gould expressed greatest concern about the third error, which may have lulled evolutionists into a false sense of security. He noted in 1983, "sadly, any hope that the issues of the *Scopes* trial had been banished to the realm of nostalgic Americana have been swept aside by our current creationist resurgence."

Yet the third part of this story had constituted the central lesson of the *Scopes* legend on which all versions concurred. The light of reason had banished religious obscurantism [opposition to the spread of knowledge]. In the 1930s, [writer, editor, and historian] Frederick Lewis Allen presented [in his 1931 book *Only Yesterday*] the *Scopes* trial as a critical watershed, after which "the slow drift away from Fundamentalist certainty continued." By the fifties, antievolutionism appeared to have safely run its course. "Today the evolution controversy seems as remote as the Homeric era [around 1200 B.C. when the Greek poet Homer lived] to intellectuals of the East," [historian Richard] Hofstadter wrote. Lawrence and Lee left no doubts about their verdict on the *Scopes* trial. When the defendant asks if he won or lost, Drummond assures everyone, "You won. . . . Millions of people will say you won. They'll read in their papers tonight that you smashed a bad law. You made it a joke!" Certainly the play's actors had no doubts about this verdict. "When we did *Inherit the Wind* in 1955, the religious right was a joke, a lunatic fringe," Tony Randall later wrote. Reviewing the movie version in 1960, *The New Republic* noted, "The Monkey Trial is now a historical curiosity, and it can be made truly meaningful only by treating it as the farce that it was." While these secular interpreters of the trial contemplated the triumph of reason, however, antievolutionism continued to build within America's growing conservative Christian subculture. As Randall ruefully observes, "Sometimes we wonder if anyone ever learns anything."

Playwrights Were Divided on the State of Freedom in 1950s America

Albert Wertheim

Albert Wertheim taught Western drama and theater at Princeton University and Indiana University before his death in 2003.

In the following article, Albert Wertheim explains how playwrights of the 1950s used their plays as tools to express their thoughts on the McCarthy era's anti-Communist witch hunts. Playwrights such as Jerome Lawrence and Robert Edwin Lee saw McCarthy's tactics as direct violations on Americans' right to think; thus Inherit the Wind *was an expression of this. Other playwrights of the time viewed communism as a direct threat to the freedoms of Americans, and their plays reflected this view. The 1950s stage, therefore, became one of divided thoughts on freedom.*

Eric Bentley's *Thirty Years of Treason*, Lillian Hellman's *Scoundrel Time*, Lately Thomas's *When Even Angels Wept*, and Robert Goldston's *The American Nightmare* are only a few of the many studies that have been written about that unsettling and aberrant period of recent American history frequently known as the McCarthy era. The very titles of the books tell us immediately with what loathing and shame most Americans now look back to that time of political paranoia. Joseph McCarthy, the junior senator from Wisconsin, who became a household word through the famous hearings that sought to excoriate Communists from the American army and from American life, was really only one aspect of a widespread

Albert Wertheim, "The McCarthy Era and the American Theatre," *Theatre Journal*, vol. 34, May 1982, pp. 211–12, 221–22. Copyright © 1982, University and College Theatre Association of the American Theatre Association. Reproduced by permission of The Johns Hopkins University Press.

fear of subversion already very much manifest long before Senator McCarthy came forth with his claims. On February 9, 1950, Senator McCarthy made his famous speech to the ladies of the Ohio County Women's Republican Club in Wheeling, West Virginia, exclaiming, "I have here in my hand a list of 205 who were known to the secretary of state as being members of the Communist Party and who, nevertheless, are still working and shaping policy in the State Department." With these words he launched his now infamous campaign against Communism, but as one historian nicely points out, the menace had merely found its spokesman. The real starting point for the so-called McCarthy era actually came several years earlier when, on March 12, 1947, President Harry S. Truman issued Executive Order 9835 creating a loyalty and security program within the American federal government.

A New Generation of Witch Hunts

Executive Order 9835 brought with it the Attorney General's List, a checklist, for internal use, of organizations with ties to Communist, Fascist and other subversive views. Were an applicant connected with any organization on the Attorney General's List, serious scrutinizing of the applicant would be in order before he or she could be placed on the federal payroll. When Truman allowed that list to be published, it became quickly used unscrupulously by an array of blacklisters: "Without charging any illegal acts, without supplying the grounds for its proscription, without offering a machinery for individual reply, the government branded as putatively disloyal any citizen who belonged to one of a large number of organizations. . . . The List, intended to supply prima facie [at first view] reason for investigating federal employees, was used to deny people employment in *any* responsible position, private or public." The main beneficiary of Executive Order 9835 was the House Un-American Activities Committee (HUAC), a then relatively insignificant committee of the House of Representatives. Young congressmen like Richard Nixon, who had been assigned to the unimportant Un-American Activities Committee saw and seized their opportunity for making it into a powerful political platform. With the "success" of the Alger Hiss [espionage] case, HUAC was launched as the machinery for expunging the Red [Communist] menace from American shores. Senator McCarthy was merely one aspect of the nightmare unleashed by President Truman's executive order and an HUAC running wild with its own power, breeding fear and hysteria in the public mind.

The period of American history colored by the Attorney General's List, by the witch-hunting of HUAC and by Senator McCarthy's infamous hearings need not be retold here nor is it necessary once again to rehearse the names and testimonies of the Hollywood and Broadway figures summoned before the HUAC and often subsequently censured or destroyed professionally. In his *Are You Now or Have You Ever Been* and *Thirty Years of Treason*, Eric Bentley has already done that for us with the eloquence of understatement. What has not, however, been given enough attention is the effect of HUAC and Joe McCarthy on American playwriting, particularly on the American drama of the early 1950s. . . .

Inherit the Wind Defends Freedom of Thought

[On] April 21, 1955, one of Broadway's most successful plays of the decade opened to near rave notices. Jerome Lawrence and Robert E. Lee's *Inherit the Wind* played to packed houses. With the names of the personages slightly changed, *Inherit the Wind* dramatizes the renowned *Scopes* Monkey Trial [a popular name for the 1925 trial that found it unlawful to teach evolution in Tennessee public schools]. In the Lawrence and Lee play, the original prosecuting attorney, William Jennings Bryan, renamed Matthew Harrison Brady, was played by Ed

Begley. The defense attorney, Clarence Darrow, renamed Henry Drummond, became one of the great roles of Paul Muni's acting career. *Inherit the Wind* is, of course, not directly about McCarthyism or the 1950s, but at the same time the impact of the play, its power, and its defense of the freedom of thought cannot be separated from the issues that divided the nation during the first years of the 50s.

The contemporary significance of *Inherit the Wind* in 1955 is stated by Lawrence and Lee in the terse preface to the play. Acknowledging the *Scopes* trial as their inspiration, they argue that theirs is not a chronicle play. "It is not 1925," they write, and the stage directions set the time as "Not too long ago. It might have been yesterday. It could be tomorrow." The implication, clearly, is that it *is* today. During the course of the play, its contemporary relevance becomes increasingly clear. In the play's trial scene, after Brady, the William Jennings Bryan character, has examined a young student of Bertram Cates, the [John] Scopes character, Brady declares with impressive courtroom rhetorical pyrotechnics:

> I say that these Bible-haters, these "Evil-utionists," are brewers of poison. And the legislature of this sovereign state has had the wisdom to demand that the peddlers of poison—in bottles or in books—clearly label the products they attempt to sell! I tell you, if this law is not upheld, this boy will become one of a generation shorn of its faith by the teachings of Godless science! But if the full penalty of the law is meted out to Bertram Cates, the faithful the whole world over, who are watching us here, and listening to our every word, will call this courtroom blessed!

One need only substitute Communism for Evolutionism and Senator McCarthy could not have put it better himself. For the audience of *Inherit the Wind*, the subject matter was novel but the rhetoric and the philosophical issue all too familiar.

Parallels Between Brady and McCarthy

Inherit the Wind is a significant play within the context of the McCarthy era, for it marks an important departure from [other] plays [of this time]. Although Bertram Cates is the evolutionist warlock that a small Tennessee town attempts to exorcize, the play does not focus on the victimization of Cates. Its gaze is, rather, on the hollowness and demagoguery of Brady. The play is Drummond's, or Paul Muni's [who won 1956 Tony Award for his performance], play as he makes increasingly evident the emptiness of Brady's rhetoric, transforming that rhetoric in the public eye to mere linguistic flatulence [gas]. By the end of *Inherit the Wind*, Brady is broken and then dies. The play thus neatly caught the tenor of the times outside the theatre. By the time *Inherit the Wind* opened, Joe McCarthy was a broken man. The tide had turned against him, as it does against Brady, and on December 2, 1954, less than five months before *Inherit the Wind* opened, the senator from Wisconsin was officially censured by the U.S. Senate. That was the death knell of his career and of the era to which he gave his name. Brady's death at the close of *Inherit the Wind* was prophetic, for exactly two and a half years after McCarthy's censure, McCarthy himself and, to a large extent, McCarthyism were laid to rest.

Theater Reflected Social Divisions

With McCarthy's censure, the Cold War paranoia was not dead, for HUAC could still try [playwright] Arthur Miller in 1956. The Communist threat is likewise present in Henry Denker and Ralph Berkey's *Time Limit!*, which opened on January 24, 1956 and featured Arthur Kennedy and Richard Kiley in the main roles. Kennedy had portrayed John Proctor in [Arthur Miller's] *The Crucible* and Kiley had played the lead in *Sing Me No Lullaby*. *Time Limit!* is about Communism and treason, but Denker and Berkey interestingly manipulate their drama so that what begins as a court martial play centering on individual subversion and treason ends as an exposé of insidious, irresistible Communist brainwashing techniques. As the main character says, "This is a new kind of enemy, sir. The code isn't equipped to deal with them." In short, the period from 1947, when HUAC assumed its power, to the demise of Senator McCarthy in 1954 marked the height of a relatively short but black period in American history. The vibrations from Washington were clearly felt everywhere in America including the American theatre and the plays it presented. And the ripple effects of those strong vibrations were felt for many years thereafter.

One would like to say that in the face of HUAC and McCarthy witch hunting American playwrights took a brave and united stand. That is not the case, but it is also not true that they yielded in a cowardly way to stage the paranoid scenarios being written in Washington. The truth of the matter is that, as it always does, the theatre reflected the divisions within society. Playwrights like Maxwell Anderson, Sidney Kingsley, Henry Denker, and Ralph Berkey clearly saw Communism and Communists as a threat to the United States and to American democracy. Others like Arthur Miller, Robert Ardrey, Lillian Hellman, James Thurber, and William Saroyan felt just as strongly that the fanatical attempt to expose Communists, former Communists and fellow travelers was more injurious to the American way of life than Communism itself. That the American stage should have been as divided on the issues as the American people themselves should come as no surprise, for, as [William] Shakespeare long ago knew, the drama and the actors "are the abstract and brief chronicles of the time."

Modern Interpretations of *Inherit the Wind*

Mark Lawson

Mark Lawson is an English journalist, author, and theater critic. Among his publications is a weekly column for The Guardian, *a major English newspaper.*

In the following selection, Lawson discusses how the significance of Inherit the Wind *has changed since its 1955 premiere. Jerome Lawrence and Robert Edwin Lee wrote* Inherit the Wind *with the intent of criticizing McCarthyism's denial of personal freedoms in its attack on Communist sympathizers. When the play premiered in 1955, the debate between creationists and evolutionists was not a matter of contemporary importance. Yet, current audiences, notes Lawson, relate the play more to the evolution-creation debate and the denial of religious freedom than to Senator Joseph McCarthy and his Communist witch hunts.*

There is a story told about many well-known foreign correspondents—Kate Adie and John Simpson especially—in which, as the reporter hands over their passport at the airport or hotel, a local does a double-take and says: "Oh God, things must be bad here." *Inherit the Wind,* . . . revived in New York [in April 2007], is the theatrical equivalent of such a pessimistic harbinger: if it turns up on Broadway, you can be sure US democracy is in trouble. Initially aimed at Senator Joseph McCarthy, architect of the 1950s anti-communist witch-hunts, the play is now directed at George W Bush.

Although premiered in 1955, the play, by Jerome Lawrence and Robert E Lee, was based on events 30 years earlier, when a Tennessee schoolteacher called [John] Scopes was tried for including [naturalist Charles] Darwin's theories [of evolution] in his science classes. In that case, William Jennings Bryan, a demagogue and frequent presidential candidate, prosecuted for the state and was opposed by Clarence Darrow, the finest trial lawyer of the day. In *Inherit the Wind*, Scopes becomes Bertram Cates, while Bryan and Darrow are lightly fictionalised as volcanic politician Matthew Harrison Brady and wily attorney Henry Drummond—bold and showy roles taken in the Broadway revival by Brian Dennehy and Christopher Plummer.

Different Meanings of "Clock-Stoppers"

The reason for these disguises, although the script closely follows the psychology of the *Scopes* trial, was that Lawrence and Lee had little interest in the creationism versus Darwinism debate, which at the time of their premiere was not a headline topic, seen more as an eccentricity from a bygone age.

When Drummond, in the work's most savage phrases, pledges to prevent "the clock-stoppers from dumping a load of medieval nonsense into the United States constitution", the authors intended their audience to think of far more recent history. Like Arthur Miller's *The Crucible* two years earlier, *Inherit the Wind* found metaphors in history to attack Senator [Joseph] McCarthy's [Senate Permanent Subcommittee on Investigations]. But one of the fascinations of revivals of famous plays is that their meaning is changed by the date of the restaging. On the night I saw the new *Inherit the Wind*, Drummond's tirade against "clock-stoppers" won applause from the New York audience, as did the liberal lawyer's later speech about "trying to stop you bigots and ignoramuses from controlling the education of the United States!"

This modern reaction was clearly not provoked by a metaphor for McCarthyism. The ticking of the clock has given the reference to "clock-stoppers" a different meaning. In a shift in the script's reception that would have surprised Lawrence and Lee, *Inherit the Wind*, never intended as a factual account of the 1925 *Scopes* trial, is likely to be seen by 2007 audiences not only as that but as a surprisingly topical defence of the teaching of Darwinism against creationist reactionaries who in contemporary America once again object to the teaching of evolution in schools. And if today's viewers do draw a wider parallel from Drummond's defence of the "constitution" against "bigots" and "clock-stoppers", then it is more likely to be with the attempts by US fundamentalists to outlaw abortion.

Shifts in Definitions of Freedom

There seems no doubt that the resurgence of Bible-justified politics in the US—under a president whose public statements suggest he may consider himself a creationist—prompted this lavish revival of a drama that had come to be seen as a play Americans of a certain age and class had read at school, and was over-shadowed by Stanley Kramer's 1960 film [version], with [actor] Spencer Tracy [as Drummond] defending science.

Although dusted off largely for non-theatrical reasons, the new production of *Inherit the Wind* serves as a perfect study of what can happen, for good or ill, to an old play in a new era. Apart from the change in the anti-creationist theme from metaphor to polemic, the new Broadway staging also reflects another more subtle shift in definitions of freedom. The published text of the play specifies that in act one "an organ-grinder enters with a live monkey on a string", and is greeted by a newspaper reporter character as "Grandpa!" In Doug Hughes's revival, the "live monkey" is a man in a hairy suit, making this creationist-baiting moment more obviously fairground burlesque. The reason is that, 50 years on, animals have been accorded an equivalence with humans that even the most diligent liberal Darwinist in 1955 could never have envisaged: the use of a live monkey today might lead to the theatre being picketed.

While biology teacher John T. Scopes was being prosecuted in Dayton, Tennessee, for teaching evolution, the Anti-Evolution League set up a book shop in the town to promote its views. © Bettmann/Corbis.

But while the play, despite this forgivable failure to anticipate animal rights, seems ideologically modern, this revival risks seeming theatrically creaky. Although *Inherit the Wind* belongs on the same thematic shelf as *The Crucible*, certainly neither playwright [i.e., Lawrence nor Lee] was an Arthur Miller; both were mostly associated with musicals. Read or seen now, *Inherit the Wind* reflects both the advantages and disadvantages of the US dramatic culture of its time. There are huge parts for star actors, building up to a heavyweight knockout bout, which the pugnacious Dennehy and feline Plummer visibly relish. And the play's scale is always impressive: it seems astonishing now that dramatists seeking a commercial production would demand a cast of 30 actors. The lavish new Broadway version often seems, to modern eyes, like a musical without songs.

Freedom Will Always Be on Trial

Although a playwright today would approach this subject with a smaller cast, they might also have bigger fists. Clearly nervous of offending too many ticket-buyers, the play carefully balances Drummond's railing against religion—"In a child's power to master the multiplication table, there is more sanctity than all your shouted Amens!"—with a later moment of reverence towards the Bible. On reflection, though, this nervous liberal tolerance of strong faith does also seem quite modern.

Seeing *Inherit the Wind* now, one speech seems oddly prophetic of its own longevity. In the final act, when the case seems to be going Drummond's way, he advises his client not to relax: "You don't suppose this kind of thing is ever finished, do you? Tomorrow it will be something else—and another fella will have to stand up".

Social Issues in Literature

CHAPTER 3

Contemporary Perspectives on Freedom of Thought

A Judge Finds No Place for Intelligent Design in Public School Curricula

David Postman

David Postman was the chief political reporter for The Seattle Times *when he wrote the following article and is now director of communications and media for Vulcan Inc., a Seattle project management firm.*

In the following article, Postman discusses the ongoing debate about intelligent design and its place in education. In December 2005 a U.S. district judge outlawed the teaching of intelligent design in a Pennsylvania school district on the constitutional basis of the separation of church and state; however, some intelligent design advocates contend that the ruling mistakenly related the theory to biblical creationism, downplaying its biological approach. Postman asserts the constitutional right of intelligent design advocates to participate in the debate with evolutionists, but he warns that some supporters are losing steam amidst the pressure to walk the middle ground between creationism and evolution.

When a federal judge stopped intelligent design from being taught in a Pennsylvania school district in December [2005] the concept's chief advocates issued a quick and pointed response.

U.S. District Judge John Jones was an activist judge whose opinion shows he's misinformed and biased, said officials at the Discovery Institute, a Seattle think tank that promotes intelligent design as a challenge to Charles Darwin's theory of evolution.

The only comfort they found in the stinging rebuke was that the ruling would carry no weight beyond Dover, Pa.

They were right in that, without an appeal to a higher court, the case sets no legal standard beyond the central Pennsylvania region where Jones' court has jurisdiction. But nearly five months after the ruling, the Discovery Institute is fighting to control fallout from the decision.

"Dover is a disaster in a sense, as a public-relations matter," said Bruce Chapman, a former Seattle city councilman and founder of the Discovery Institute, the country's primary supporter of intelligent design. "It has given a rhetorical weapon to the Darwinists to say a judge has settled this," he said.

Even some critics of evolution have taken the ruling as a sign that the fight to bring intelligent design into public schools may be over.

Where Intelligent Design Stands

Intelligent design argues that life is so biologically complex, there must be some kind of supernatural designer involved. The concept, however, leaves the designer unnamed.

Chapman said the ruling, which equated intelligent design with biblically based creationism, has been misread by opponents and backers of intelligent design.

"We have problems on both sides," he said. "There is no doubt that many conservatives and liberals alike—if they have not studied the matter—mix up the science issue with religion."

Already, he said, an effort in Ohio to include intelligent design in school curricula failed when some state school-board members said the Dover case settled the issue.

Leading conservative commentators—including talk-radio host Rush Limbaugh and syndicated columnist Cal Thomas—say the judge's decision shows that intelligent design is a failed strategy in the effort to bring religion into the public schools.

"Let's make no mistake," Limbaugh said on his radio show. "The people pushing intelligent design believe in the biblical version of creation. Intelligent design is a way, I think, to sneak it into the curriculum and make it less offensive to the liberals."

Still, the publicity hasn't been all bad, said Stephen Meyer, director of the Discovery Institute's Center for Science and Culture, which produces studies and reports about intelligent design.

"The ACLU [American Civil Liberties Union] sued to keep a few students in Pennsylvania from hearing about intelligent design, and as a result, they made sure everyone in the world heard about it," Meyer said. "And that has not hurt us."

But there is a lesson in Dover, where Chapman and Meyer said the School Board hijacked intelligent-design terminology for its attempt to bring religion into school. Chapman said Discovery told the board not to attempt to teach intelligent design. Instead, he said, the institute advocates that schools only "teach the controversy" surrounding evolution.

"We're mostly trying to stop people from doing dumb things," Meyer said.

To that end, the institute this month [April 2006] published *Traipsing into Evolution: Intelligent Design and the* Kitzmiller vs. Dover *Decision*, a book critiquing Jones' decision in the Dover Area School District case.

"Our role was widely misconstrued by both sides—and the media," Chapman said. "So we want to set the record straight."

Creationism vs. Intelligent Design

Intelligent design argues that evolution leaves major gaps in understanding the origins of life, gaps that can only be explained by the presence of a supernatural designer.

Discovery Institute scientists say, for example, that the genetic code embedded in DNA is so complicated it couldn't possibly be the result of natural selection.

Creationists believe God made the universe and all life within it. The Discovery Institute says intelligent design is different in that it uses science to argue that some kind of unidentified designer must have been at work.

"Although I find it congenial to think that it's God, others might prefer to think it's an alien—or who knows? An angel, or some satanic force, some new age power," Michael Behe, a leading Discovery fellow, said in a British newspaper last year.

The ACLU teamed up with locals in Dover to sue the School Board for teaching intelligent design, which they said violated the separation of church and state.

After a six-week trial, Jones concluded the "overwhelming evidence" showed intelligent design "is a religious view, a mere relabeling of creationism." He added that there was no real science to back up the concept.

Even some Christian critics of evolution didn't like what they heard about intelligent design.

Paul Chesser, an editor at a North Carolina free market think tank, the John Locke Foundation, calls intelligent design a "diluted account of Creation." He wonders why it left out God.

"Why do Christians wage combat over taking Christ out of Christmas but employ weak dodge-and-parry tactics when educating their kids about life's beginnings?" Chesser wrote in a column headlined "Cowering Christians."

Columnist Thomas, a former spokesman for the conservative Christian political group Moral Majority, said the court decision shows that academic debates, lawsuits and alternate explanations are not the way to fight the secularization of the United States.

"It should awaken religious conservatives to the futility of trying to make a secular state reflect their beliefs," Thomas wrote.

Hugh Ross, president of Reasons to Believe, a group that says it provides "Bible-based and scientifically testable evidence to support the accuracy of the Scriptures," considers himself a Discovery Institute ally. His California foundation promotes an old-earth creation concept. Ross believes the universe started billions of years ago with the big bang, as many cosmologists theorize, but said God intervened throughout history to create all life on Earth.

Ross said the Discovery Institute is hampered by its attempt to walk a middle ground between evolution and creationism. By doing that, he said, "you make theology weak and you make science weak."

His advice: Acknowledge that God is the designer. "We're just saying, 'You guys need to go a lot farther than you're going, You've got to quit ducking the issue.'"

Seeking Middle Ground

Chapman said his interest in academic freedom led him to expand the Discovery Institute's mandate in 1996 from transportation, technology and education to include a challenge to evolution.

He was bothered that teachers were reluctant to discuss intelligent design in public schools and that university researchers weren't encouraged to study it.

And while he promotes intelligent design with fervor, he said he wants to build a dispassionate middle ground in the debate between creationism and evolution.

"It's a very narrow path," said Brian Ogilvie, who teaches the history of science at the University of Massachusetts, Amherst. He is writing a book on the history of various intelligent-design arguments.

Conservative talk radio host Rush Limbaugh believes intelligent design is a way to sneak biblical creationism into school curricula in a less offensive manner. © Jim Sulley/epa/ Corbis.

When intelligent-design proponents speak to Christian audiences, "there's no question about who the designer is," Ogilvie said. "They've adopted the strategy of saying one thing to the faithful and another one to the scientific community."

Discovery Institute funders, including the Maclellan Foundation in Chattanooga, Tennessee, have open religious agendas. Another donor, the Stewardship Foundation of Tacoma, says it "provides resources to Christ-centered organizations whose mission is to share their faith in Jesus Christ." Its founder, the late David Weyerhaeuser, was also interested in science, Meyer said.

Leading Discovery Institute fellows also are clear they think God is the designer.

Chapman said he asked Discovery fellows not to testify in the *Dover* case. But Scott Minnich, a microbiologist, and Michael Behe, a biochemistry professor, did and were asked in court who they thought the designer was.

"The designer is in fact God," Behe testified.

Minnich, said he thought the intelligent agent is the God of Christianity. He added that was his "personal opinion, but that's not based on a scientific conclusion."

William Dembski, a leading Discovery Institute fellow, has written that intelligent design "opens the path for people to come to Christ."

Chapman said the scientists were discussing their personal religious beliefs, which shouldn't be confused with the Discovery Institute's conclusions based on scientific evidence.

That distinction can be hard for people to understand.

"You can be so nuanced people lose the point," said Richard Thompson, president and chief counsel of the Thomas More Law Center in Ann Arbor, Michigan, a public-interest law firm that represented Dover school-board members against the ACLU.

"They can't understand what you're doing and why you're saying what you're saying, and that might be the problem with the Discovery Institute," Thompson said.

Critiquing the Judge

The Discovery Institute's new book is 123 pages of critique and references aimed at disputing Jones' decision.

At the heart of the criticism is the institute's position that Jones blindly accepted Darwin's theory while ignoring what it says is scientific evidence of intelligent design.

Chapman said that to criticize intelligent design because some of its promoters are religious is unfair, given that atheism among "Darwinists" goes unmentioned.

He said the judge tried to cripple debate over evolution and make it appear there was a "diabolical plot" to undermine the Constitution.

Chapman explains Jones' logic this way: Criticizing Darwin's theory amounts to intelligent design in disguise. And because intelligent design is a way to sneak creationism—and therefore religion—into schools, that criticism isn't allowed.

Jones, in his decision, anticipated the critique from intelligent-design supporters.

"Those who disagree with our holding will likely mark it as the product of an activist judge," he wrote. "If so they have erred as this is manifestly not an activist court."

Quebec Should Not Mandate a Course in Ethics and Religious Culture

Jean Morse-Chevrier

Jean Morse-Chevrier is president of the Association of Catholic Parents of Quebec.

In the following piece, Morse-Chevrier voices distress over Quebec's 2005 adoption of Bill 95, which imposed a new course on every school and every student in the Canadian province of Quebec. The course, Ethics and Religious Culture, exposes students to all religious beliefs, including Christian, Buddhist, and Muslim, treating them as equally valid. Among other things, the course is intended to encourage students to respect and get along with those of all faiths. Morse-Chevrier argues that the bill denies parents their right to shape their children's faith-based education.

Since September 2008, a new course of Ethics and Religious Culture (ERC) has been introduced into all Quebec schools, from grade one to the end of high school. Parents have been up in arms about this course since the Quebec government first made known its preliminary version in the fall of 2006. At that time, the Ministry of Education requested the Quebec Assembly of Catholic Bishops, the Association of Catholic Parents of Quebec, and other religious groups give their opinions on the contents to the Committee for Religious Affairs.

As President of the Association of Catholic Parents of Quebec, I was outraged that, following the consultation, parents' opinions were ignored. All parents consulted by the association had expressed their definite desire to maintain their right to oversee the courses. After all, its religious and moral content would be transmitted to their children.

A Denial of Parents' Rights

The Quebec Charter of Human Rights and Freedoms recognized the responsibility of the schools to respect parents' beliefs and convictions within school programs. That changed drastically in June 2005, with the adoption of Bill 95. The National Assembly, without previous debate, agreed unanimously to withdraw that provision from the Quebec charter.

Since the summer of 2005, parents have suffered from a total lack of regard. The government has shown a total lack of respect for parental rights to determine the moral and religious education of their children. First, the course was imposed equally on private denominational schools and public schools, with the only difference being that private schools may also teach religious education of their choice besides the course of Ethics and Religious Culture. Then, the Minister of Education, Jean-Marc Fournier, later followed by Michelle Courchesne, declared that no exemptions would be allowed.

Most of Quebec's private schools are Catholic; some others are of various Christian denominations, or of Jewish or Muslim faith. That has not stopped most of these schools from caving in to the government's demand. The one exception is English-language Loyola High School, which has begun a court challenge.

Most private schools are subsidized for a little more than half their costs by the government. But even non-subsidized private schools are forced to give the course. Parents, therefore, have nowhere to turn. Objecting are mostly Catholic, as well as some other Christian or atheist parents.

A Battle of Schools and Families

Before 2006, Catholics and Protestants had a choice of moral and religious education according to their faith; those without religious affiliation had the option of a course of moral education without religious content. Now, these families have lost the option of a course according to their beliefs. But what infuriates the parents the most is the fact that the Quebec government is subjecting their children to the teaching of faiths that are incompatible with their own.

Approximately 1,400 families have requested that their children be exempt from this course; all public schools have officially refused, backed by their school boards, which, by law, have the right to grant such exemptions. Because of the Minister's stand, school boards refuse to exercise that right. Backed into a corner, some parents have withdrawn their children from the course, in spite of the school's refusal. Many others have not dared to go that far or even to request an exemption.

In J.H. Leclerc senior high school in Granby, the principal suspended six male students from classes for a day, just before Christmas, after they had missed 20 classes of the new course. This caused a frenzy in the media. The students, all evangelical, have continued to absent themselves from the course. Diane Gagne, mother of one of the boys, expects a second suspension to kick in soon, this time for a period of two days. In the event of renewed absences, the school plans to increase the length of suspensions gradually up to 4 days. After 35 missed periods, according to what is called the life code of the school, the students will be expelled from school. Mrs. Gagne contends that the children are pretty shaken up by the school's actions but are determined to stand their ground, as are the parents. Lawyer Jean-Yves Cote has sent a letter of "putting in default" to the school demanding that students be allowed to attend their mandatory classes needed for the high school diploma.

Awaiting Courts' Decisions

Mr. Cote is requesting a temporary injunction against the application of the sanctions of J.H. Leclerc's life code, with the intent of obtaining a judgment on whether the absences are motivated. The school argues that they are not, in applying its disciplinary measures. If an injunction is granted, students would be allowed to attend all classes until the maximum of 35 absences was reached. Then, if the judge did not agree that there was motive for withdrawal from class, the students would be expelled from school. In Granby's junior high school, L'Envolee, in early January [2009], two female evangelical students were required to attend school on a professional development day to make up the time they missed by skipping ERC classes. Other schools in Granby tolerate students' absences and have chosen not to fight parents' decisions, according to Ms. Gagne.

Elsewhere in the province, schools are tolerating student boycotts of the class. In Valcourt's primary school, in the Eastern Townships, about 20 students are skipping their ERC class as well as another 3 in high school, according to one of the parents, Sylvain Lamontagne. Four of the primary school students are taken from class by volunteers who keep them occupied while the rest stay with family members. In Beauceville, another 20 students are boycotting the class at the primary level and another 10 to 20 students are skipping the class in high school. In St-Georges at Notre-Dame-de-la-Trinite high school, about 50 students are staying away from the class. Many others throughout the territory of the Beauce Etchemin school board don't attend the class. According to Jean Trottier, a parent and spokesman for the Coalition for Freedom in Education, many students attend class much against their will for lack of ability to make other arrangements during the class period. According to him, the school board has not been grading the course for absentees and is awaiting a decision on the part of the Ministry of Education on how to proceed. In most areas of Quebec, schools and school boards are waiting to see what the courts will decide.

Appeals to the Courts

There is a court case scheduled to be heard from the 11th to the 13th of May, 2009, in Quebec's Superior Court in Drummondville. Two Catholic parents are challenging the school's refusal of an exemption for both their first grader and their sixteen-year-old who is in last year of high school. They are arguing that the course's content puts their children's faith at risk. This will most likely be a test case for Quebec parents. The lawyer representing the parents, Jean-Yves Cote, hoped that the judge would rule the school board's decisions unacceptable on the grounds that they had not exercised their right to grant exemptions. The judge has rejected arguments on those grounds.

The lawyer also appealed to the fact that, in principle, all religious and moral education done in schools should satisfy parental requirements. But the judge has indicated that he wishes to hear the arguments that would demonstrate that the parents' and children's right to freedom of religion and conscience are curtailed by the application of the law that makes this course mandatory. The lawyer has a monumental task in front of him, and this court case can rightly be called a constitutional challenge to Bill 95, a bill that removed options in religious education, imposed one mandatory course of ethics and religious culture and removed from the Quebec charter the parental right to oversee school programs. [The parents lost the May 2009 court case.]

The Bishops' Perspectives

In March 2007, Cardinal Marc Ouellet of Quebec expressed the opinion that parents should maintain the right to oversee programs with religious and moral contents, and that they should have the choice of a program in accordance with their faith and convictions. He reported that the Quebec Assembly of Catholic Bishops did not want to see the course imposed on private Catholic schools. Then in March 2008, the Quebec Assembly of Catholic Bishops made known its majority position, vis-a-vis the new course, in a press release, a letter to the Minister of Education, and a Declaration. The bishops expressed a preference for respect of parental rights in the choice of the moral and religious education of their children. They expressed reservations and fears about the impact the course would have on children, on their attitude toward religion and on their faith. They stated that in order to warrant an exemption, the reasons should be serious, such as the violation of freedom of conscience which they do not consider is at risk by the program.

They state that their position is one of "critical vigilance." They argue that the program should be implemented gradually in order to prevent undesired effects. They suggest that the Quebec government evaluate the impact of the course in three to five years. They suggest that if, at that time, the negative effects outweigh the positive, another undetermined option should be offered. They express their intention to remain attentive to the impact of the program; for example, by putting in place a committee of experts who would follow the implementation of the program and receive observations through the dioceses based on experience.

Experiences in the Classroom

The Coalition for Freedom in Education, on the other hand, backed by the Association of Catholic Parents of Quebec, and by Orthodox, Melkite, Evangelical, Pentecostal and other Christian groups, has asked parents to inform them of their experiences in the classroom. Since the summer of 2007, this group and its supporters have held demonstrations, marches, press conferences and participated in many media events, interviews, and talk shows in order to keep the public informed, support the parents and put pressure on the Quebec government. However, the government has shown no signs of giving in. The only leader who showed a political inclination to have parents' views respected, Mario Dumont, lost badly in the last provincial election, whereas the Liberal and Parti Quebecois parties who were instrumental in forcing the course on parents, both made significant gains.

In the meantime, publishers have been churning out school books for children, teaching guides for teachers and audio-visual material for classes in Ethics and Religious Culture. Different sets of didactic material are now available for grades one through six, but at the high school level, school books have been longer in coming; some are expected to be available in the fall of 2009. Parents have had some access to school books for the children but the material intended for teachers is prohibitively expensive. Radio-Canada radio and television have also aired live episodes of ERC classes. Parents' fears have been confirmed by what they have seen and heard and they continue to have many objections to the material itself and to the way the program requires that it be taught.

Exposure to Multiple Beliefs

Beginning with grade one, children are exposed to religious stories, practices and beliefs of numerous religions: Christianity, Judaism, Islam, Hinduism, Buddhism and others as well as native spiritualities and atheistic world visions are jumbled together. Different schools choose different manuals and it is difficult to know which ones are most prevalent.

One series that seems quite popular is published by Modulo and seems to be fairly representative. Christianity is portrayed as just another religious story where Jesus is a figure comparable to Mohammed or Buddha, for example. His divine nature is omitted, as is his mission of salvation for all mankind. His resurrection is played down. Christian teachings and Gospel passages find their place alongside native mythology and Muslim, Hindu or other religious beliefs. There is nothing to support children in their Christian beliefs.

In fact, quite the opposite is true because course content on the various religions is often presented in class by the children themselves after they have researched a topic or story. The accent is on listening to the positions or experiences of all peoples without judging.

Yet, at the same time, the program specifies that children be questioned about whether their own beliefs have changed or not and be able to justify their position. They are also given a series of criteria for exercising good judgment, with observation and reason taking a front seat and revelation totally absent.

The ethics part of the course concentrates on how to get along first with those who are closest to the child, then gradually with all peoples. The religious characteristics are part of what children are required to get along with. All beliefs are portrayed at the outset as equally valid and the search for religious truth is not among the objectives of the course.

A Disappointing Lack of Support

As you can well see the Catholic Parents' Association cannot and will not accept the imposition of multiple religions, world views and moral positions, taught in a relativistic manner, on young children and adolescents alike. The Association defends the child's right to receive teachings about Christ and to practise his religion without the interference of the state. It also defends the rights of parents to refuse teachings in school that jeopardize their children's religious and moral education.

The stand of the Quebec Assembly of Catholic Bishops' Conference, in our opinion, is disappointing to most parents who hoped to have the backing of their pastors when trying to defend their children's faith. They feel abandoned because the bishops do not support those of them who have requested exemptions or withdrawn their children from the course. This stand by the bishops is interpreted as a lack of respect for parental rights. Parents also object to the fact that the bishops suggest waiting 3 to 5 years before the course is formally evaluated because they fear that the damage will already be done to their children by then. Nor do they agree to leave it up to the Quebec government, whose secularist bureaucrats have created this new mandatory State religion, to make the judgement as to whether the Catholic faith of the children has been harmed.

Parents also feel that a laissez-faire attitude towards the course is a betrayal of Catholic doctrine and principles. The universal Church has always held that parental rights over their children's education is part of the natural law.

In fact Canon Law renders parents responsible for making sure that their children receive moral and religious education in schools that respect the child's freedom of conscience and for giving their children Catholic schooling when possible.

Fortunately, Cardinal Marc Ouellet has expressed his opposition to the imposition of this course, to the removal of options in moral and religious education and to the trampling of parental rights. The papal nuncio [the Vatican's government representative in Canada], Mgr [Monsignor] Luigi Ventura, also has expressed his belief that the course does not respect the Canadian Charter of Rights and Freedoms.

He objects to the fact that the State is imposing a secular religion wherein no religion can be recognized as containing the truth.

Freedom of Expression in Books Comes at a Cost

David L. Ulin

David L. Ulin is editor of the Los Angeles Times Book Review.

Ulin discusses the 2008 Banned Books Week in the selection that follows. He asserts his understanding of those who would protect freedom of expression for every voice, but meanwhile he cannot deny the real dangers that some books pose. Ulin gives the examples of Thomas Paine's Common Sense, *which inspired the American Revolution, and Adolf Hitler's* Mein Kampf, *which inspired the formation of Nazi Germany. He maintains that some books continue to have the social and political power to change the course of culture for better or for worse. In short, Ulin believes the implications of freedom of expression are more complicated than Banned Books Week might suggest.*

I'm ambivalent about Banned Books Week .... On the one hand, we clearly still need such a public affirmation, as the recent tumult over [Republican vice presidential candidate] Sarah Palin and her "rhetorical" inquiries to the Wasilla, Alaska, public library show.

On the other, Banned Books Week offers up the sort of toothless, feel-good spectacle that makes us less likely to consider the actual ramifications of free expression.

The basic message here is one of astonishment: Why would anyone ban books when literature is such a positive and ennobling force? Yet while I agree with that, I also believe that some books truly *are* dangerous, and to ignore that is simply disingenuous.

We Cannot Strip Books of Their Power

Lest this make me seem an apologist for the book banners, nothing could be further from the truth. In fact, I'm against restricting anything other than material that graphically portrays certain illegal acts.

Yet it's foolish, self-defeating even, to pretend that books are innocuous, that we don't need to concern ourselves with what they say. If that's the case, then it doesn't really matter if we ban them, because we have already stripped them of their power.

Books do change things: Just think of *Common Sense* [by American revolutionary Thomas Paine], which lighted the fuse of the American Revolution, or [Adolf Hitler's] *Mein Kampf*, which laid out the blueprint for Hitler's Germany.

These are very different books—one a work of hope and human decency, the other as venal a piece of writing as I've ever read—but what they have in common is a kind of historical imperative, the sense that, at the right place and time, a book can be a galvanizing factor, for good or ill.

Mein Kampf is a title you don't hear a lot during Banned Books Week; the focus is more on classics such as [Toni Morrison's] *Song of Solomon* or [J.D. Salinger's] *The Catcher in the Rye* that have been challenged in libraries and schools.

That's understandable, but again, it reduces the territory of censorship and free expression to something neatly clarified, rather than the ambiguous morass it is. What happens when our ideals require us to defend a piece of writing that is reprehensible, that stands against everything we stand for?

It's easy to condemn those who would remove *The Adventures of Huckleberry Finn* [by Mark Twain] from a library, but what about *The Turner Diaries* [by white separatist William Luther Pierce] or *The Protocols of the Elders of Zion* [a text that promotes global domination by Jewish people]? Or for that matter, *Tintin in the Congo* [a comic strip by Hergé],

Pages from an Arabic edition of Adolf Hitler's Mein Kampf. *David L. Ulin maintains that some books, like this one, have the power to change the course of history for the worse.* © Hulton-Deutsch Collection/Corbis.

which [publisher] Little, Brown dropped from its *Tintin* reissue series last fall after controversy arose about the book's racist overtones?

These are not just academic questions; they are the heart of the matter, regardless of where you stand on the ideological divide. How do we defend one book without defending all? Such a notion can't help but make us uneasy, but then, that's one of the most essential things books can do.

Confronting Books' Opposing Views

We read for many reasons—to be educated, entertained, illuminated, challenged—but more than anything to confront someone else's ideas. Much of the time, this is miraculous: I think of all the books that have transformed me, that literally changed the way I thought.

What would my life have been like if I had never encountered Kurt Vonnegut, or read Joan Didion's *Slouching Towards Bethlehem*, the first book ever to make me think of nonfiction as a literary art?

Yet we forget the world is complicated, that it is full of opposing viewpoints and beliefs that, in many cases, we can't accommodate, at our own peril. What to do, then? Sweep them under the rug? Or face them and consider what we're up against?

This is the conversation we ought to be having during Banned Books Week, a conversation that encompasses not just a love of reading and a disdain for those who would restrict it but also the implications of the free flow of ideas. Even the most horrific things have something to teach us, something about human darkness, our capacity to go wrong.

I was thinking about this recently while reading Irvine Welsh's new novel, *Crime*, which deals with a ring of pedophiles. It's a squeamish, tricky read, and yet, like other writers who deal with transgressive or repugnant material, Welsh has a larger moral vision: His story is not about sex but sensibility, an investigation into the twisted landscape of the soul. There are those who'd argue that the subject he explores in *Crime* is not just provocative but detrimental, something we'd be better off without.

I couldn't agree less; the more troublesome a piece of writing, the more we need to take it into account.

"[T]he peculiar evil of silencing the expression of an opinion," John Stuart Mill wrote in *On Liberty* (in a quote featured on the American Library Association website), "is that it is robbing the human race; posterity as well as the existing generation; those who dissent from the opinion, still more than those who hold it. If the opinion is right, they are deprived of the opportunity of exchanging error for truth: if wrong, they lose, what is almost as great a benefit, the clearer perception and livelier impression of truth, produced by its collision with error."

Here we have the point entirely, for if books don't make us uncomfortable, they're not doing their job.

To call that a mixed blessing is an understatement in a world where a work like *Mein Kampf* can continue to exert its awful pull. And yet to suggest otherwise is to declare that writing is unessential, which is even worse.

The Patriot Act Allows for Unconstitutional Search and Seizure

Los Angeles Times

The Los Angeles Times *is the nation's second largest daily newspaper.*

The following editorial from the Los Angeles Times *evaluates the USA Patriot Act as the act approaches its expiration date at the end of 2009. After the terrorist attacks of September 11, 2001, the Uniting and Strengthening America by Providing Appropriate Tools Required to Intercept and Obstruct Terrorism Act, most often referred to simply as the Patriot Act, was put in place to strengthen national security and prevent future terrorist acts. The* Times *argues that, while some provisions of the act are necessary and just, others cut constitutional corners and trespass on citizens' right to privacy. Comparing the act to the aggressive anti-Communist investigations led by Senator Joseph McCarthy in the 1950s, the viewpoint asserts that the Patriot Act has allowed for searches and seizures without adequate justification that such intrusions are supporting the war on terrorism. The* Times *argues for greater transparency regarding some of the act's unconventional allowances and says that the government must find a reasonable balance between national security and the protection of constitutionally guaranteed privacy.*

A long with the Guantanamo Bay detention facility and the [George W.] Bush administration's illegal eavesdropping on U.S. citizens, the USA Patriot Act came to symbolize the excesses of the post-9/11 war on terrorism. Now, as it weighs the extension of three expiring provisions, the Democratic-controlled Congress has an opportunity to restore key privacy protections that were forgotten in the aftermath of the attacks.

Earlier this month [October 2009], the Senate Judiciary Committee approved a bill to renew the provisions and sent it to the Senate floor. Unfortunately, though the bill is an improvement over current law, it still falls short. The full Senate and House, where an extension bill was introduced last week, can do better.

The USA Patriot Act, supported by members of Congress from both parties and signed by President George W. Bush only 6 ½ weeks after 9/11, is formally known as the Uniting and Strengthening America by Providing Appropriate Tools Required to Intercept and Obstruct Terrorism Act of 2001. The grandiose title, like the law's hasty enactment, reflected the national resolve to do something, anything, to prevent a repeat of 9/11.

The Patriot Act's Give and Take

Some parts of the original act were relatively uncontroversial, including those permitting the CIA [Central Intelligence Agency] and the FBI [Federal Bureau of Investigation] to share information more freely and allowing investigators to seek warrants for "roving wiretaps" targeted at individuals rather than telephone numbers. Others, however, unjustifiably eroded privacy rights. Particularly troubling were rules governing the acquisition of financial and other records that allowed investigators to conduct fishing expeditions—as long as the documents were deemed "relevant" to a search for terrorists.

In December [2009], three provisions of the Patriot Act are set to expire: those dealing with roving wiretaps and the acquisition of records, and another (added in 2004) that allows surveillance of what are known as "lone wolf" terrorist suspects. All three extensions strike us as reasonable, though in one case further privacy protections are essential.

According to a Los Angeles Times *editorial, the USA Patriot Act—put in place after the terrorist attacks of September 11, 2001—has allowed for unjust searches and seizures and has shown that there needs to be more of a balance between national security and the protection of constitutional rights.* © Reuters NewMedia Inc./Corbis.

In the era of disposable cellphones, it makes sense for investigators, with a court order, to be able to listen in on a targeted suspect's calls regardless of where he is. And roving wiretaps long have been used in criminal investigations.

More problematic is the provision allowing court orders for business records and other "tangible things"—popularly known as the "library records" provision because of fears that investigators would monitor the reading habits of citizens (even though the law doesn't mention library records specifically). The Judiciary Committee bill explicitly makes it harder to obtain library records and requires investigators to show a court that the material sought is reasonably likely to be relevant to an intelligence investigation. Under current law, by contrast, a judge is supposed to presume that the materials are relevant. Even with that refinement, "relevance to an investigation" is too loose a standard for a court order. As "Senators" Russell D. Feingold (D-Wis.) and Richard J. Durbin (D-Ill.) proposed, the bill should be revised to require a tighter connection to a particular foreign agent or terrorist.

Finally, the bill would extend the lone wolf provision, under which investigators can seek a warrant to spy on a suspected terrorist even if he is not affiliated with a foreign power or organized terrorist group. Critics argue that this provision—which the [Barack] Obama administration says has never been employed—is unnecessary because any suspected terrorist acting alone could be investigated under criminal laws. True, but the collection of foreign intelligence had previously been subject to rules different from those of a criminal investigation. On balance, the committee was right to extend this provision. Not every foreign terrorist is a card-carrying member of Al Qaeda and thus is not always so easily spotted and monitored.

Abusing Search and Seizure

The Patriot Act's greatest threat to personal privacy lies not in any of the provisions set to expire but in the law's expansion of the use of national security letters, subpoenas that allow the FBI to obtain records without a warrant. In 2008, the FBI issued 24,744 letters involving the records of 7,225 people. Not surprisingly, there have been abuses. In 2007, after an investigation of four FBI offices, the Justice Department's inspector general found irregularities in 22% of documents related to the issuance of national security letters. Last year [2008], he found that the FBI had made "significant progress" in correcting violations.

Even so, the criteria for issuing the letters are too vague. At present, the government must merely certify that the information sought is relevant to an authorized investigation. The bill approved by the Judiciary Committee would increase the burden on the government slightly by requiring a written statement of specific facts demonstrating relevance. A narrower amendment by Feingold and Durbin—which would have required issuance of national security letters to be related to a suspected foreign agent or terrorist or a possible confederate—was rejected by the committee. It should be added on the Senate floor or in an eventual conference with the House.

The other problem with national security letters is that the companies or other institutions that receive them are not allowed to reveal that fact publicly, though they can appeal them in a closed hearing in federal District Court. Feingold proposed that the government certify that disclosure of the request would result in serious harm, and that the gag be lifted in a year's time unless the government presented new evidence that secrecy was necessary. The final version of the Patriot Act extension legislation should include those safeguards.

The committee also approved new limits on "sneak and peek" searches of a property conducted in the absence of the owner or resident. Currently, the targets of such searches must be informed within 30 days after the search; the committee reduced that to seven days.

It's easy amid this welter of technical provisions to lose sight of the overarching question: To what degree can invasions of privacy be justified by the need to investigate and prevent acts of terrorism? In the aftermath of 9/11, both Congress and the executive branch needlessly cut legal corners. It's time to make amends.

Scholars of Middle East Studies Are Victims of the New McCarthyism

Larry Cohler-Esses

The editor at large for the New York City community paper The Jewish Week *when he wrote the following article, Larry Cohler-Esses is currently assistant managing editor of* The Jewish Daily Forward, *a renowned independent community newspaper also based in New York.*

In the following essay, Cohler-Esses introduces a string of cases where academics involved in Middle East studies were slandered by the media and then denied tenure or dismissed altogether. Cohler-Esses attributes these injustices to a modern McCarthyism—originally named for the rampant accusations of Communist sympathy by Senator Joseph McCarthy and his supporters in the 1950s. This renewed phenomenon, says the author, depends first on public outrage over alleged radical inclinations and opposition to Israel, with the result of government and donor pressure on academic departments to deny their employees career stability.

Meet Professor Nadia Abu El-Haj, a notorious Barnard College professor now up for tenure who:

- claims the ancient Israelite kingdoms are a "pure political fabrication,"
- denies the Romans destroyed Jerusalem in 70 CE [common era] and instead blames its destruction on the Jews,

- does not speak or read Hebrew yet had the temerity to publish a book on Israeli archaeology that demanded such expertise,

- is so ignorant of her topic that she quotes one archaeologist on how a dig might have damaged the ancient palaces of Solomon—oblivious to the fact that those palaces, if they existed, were far from the site in question.

None of these charges are true. You could look it up. I did, in El-Haj's book *Facts on the Ground*, about which these charges are made. The statements for which a network of right-wing critics assail her book are not there.

Questioning the Critics' Integrity

I asked Paula Stern, the Barnard alum who has organized an online petition demanding that El-Haj be denied tenure, how she squared her petition's charges with El-Haj's book. "The petition takes pieces of criticisms from experts. It may not be quoted 100 percent accurate," she admitted. Still, more than 2,500 people, including many Barnard and Columbia alumni, have signed on to its claims. Tellingly, Stern, who now lives in the West Bank, voiced astonishment at being asked to justify her charges in terms of what El-Haj's book actually says. "I've spoken to many newspapers," she said. "No one has done what you've done."

I looked that up, too. In the key media venues, at least, Stern was right; and not just with regard to her target. In case after case, a network of right-wing activists has started an online furor based on a mélange of distorted or provably false charges against someone involved in Middle East studies. They supported these charges with quotes yanked out of context or entirely made up and wielded a broad brush of guilt by association. Right-wing media megaphoned the charges, stoking the furor. And mainstream media ultimately noticed and responded, often focusing their stories on the furor rather than the facts.

Under pressure from these assaults, some academic institutions buckle and a professor's career is derailed; in other cases it is permanently stained. More insidious, even when tenure puts an academic beyond the reach of his or her assailants, more vulnerable junior faculty and grad students take note. "There certainly is a sense among faculty and grad students that they're being watched, monitored," said Zachary Lockman, president of the Middle East Studies Association. "People are always looking over their shoulder, feeling that whatever they say—in accurate or, more likely, distorted form—can end up on a website. It definitely has a chilling effect."

This is the modus operandi of the New McCarthyism. It targets a new enemy for our era: Muslims, Arabs and others in the Middle East field who are identified as stepping over an unstated line in criticizing Israel, as radical Islamists, as just plain radical or as in some way sympathetic to terrorists. Its purveyors include Campus Watch, run by Arab studies scholar Daniel Pipes; the David Project, supported by the Charles and Lynn Schusterman Foundation; and David Horowitz's *FrontPage Magazine* (in October [2007] Horowitz organized an "Islamo-Fascism Awareness Week" on campuses across the nation).

A Conspiracy

Their efforts often appear to be linked. As first noted by blogger Richard Silverstein, the earliest web attack on El-Haj's book was posted simultaneously by Campus Watch and *FrontPage*, in October 2005. Alexander Joffe, identified as a professor at SUNY [State University of New York], Purchase, published a harshly negative review of the book in *The Journal of Near Eastern Studies* that same month. The prestigious journal did not note—and was not informed—that he was then director of Campus Watch. Soon after, he became research director for the David Project. Less prominent researchers like Stern, the online *PipeLine News* and writers such as Beila Rabinowitz and William Mayer provide raw material to the more well-known portals, such as Pipes and Horowitz. Pipes's and Horowitz's material is, in turn, picked up by key conservative papers like the *New York Post* and *New York Sun*.

There is an undeniable security threat, but as in the 1950s the New McCarthyites use it as a base for demagogy. Their distinguishing feature is not concern about this threat but cynical indifference to the truth or decency of their charges. Take the case of Debbie Almontaser, the New York City public high school principal forced to resign in August [2007] as head of a new Arabic/English secondary school. The furor revolved around her attempt in an interview with the *Post* to explain the meaning of, rather than simply condemn, T-shirts bearing the words Intifada NYC. This provoked a firestorm. United Federation of Teachers chief Randi Weingarten, a key supporter of Almontaser's school, condemned her in a letter to the *Post*. The next day Almontaser resigned—a move publicly welcomed by Schools Chancellor Joel Klein and Mayor Michael Bloomberg. Almontaser has since stated she was told to resign or the school, which she founded, would be closed.

In its obscuring, anodyne [unfeeling] postmortem on the affair, the *New York Times* vaguely described Almontaser as a victim of the city's "treacherous ethnic and ideological political currents" rather than of specific charges that were demonstrably false—like Pipes's widely publicized claim, based on a truncated quotation, that she denied Muslims or Arabs were involved in the 9/11 [terrorist] attacks. The *Times* report on El-Haj adopted a similar hands-off stance, simply quoting supporters and attackers. It did not once compare the activists' charges with what El-Haj actually said in her book.

As it happens, Almontaser's forced resignation was the city Education Department's second dive in the face of pressure from the New McCarthyites. Three years ago it dismissed Professor Rashid Khalidi, the esteemed director of Columbia's Middle East Institute, from lecturing teachers enrolled in professional development courses. The dismissal came in response to a *Sun* article claiming Khalidi had denounced Israel as "a 'racist' state with an 'apartheid system.'" Khalidi denied the quote fragments as they were used in the story. "I do not think Zionism is racist," he told the *Forward*. "When we talk about some of the contemporary laws, there are policies that I consider racist and discriminatory." Asked if the department had verified Khalidi's purported remarks before dismissing him, a department spokesman avoided answering *Times* columnist Joyce Purnick.

Fueled by Public Outrage

Khalidi still has his day job, as does—so far—a nontenured Columbia colleague, Joseph Massad, who according to a special school investigative committee was falsely accused several years ago of discriminating against Jewish and Israeli students. The same cannot be said for Norman Finkelstein, who was terminated at Chicago's DePaul University in September after the school's president—in a rare departure from standard procedure—rejected the overwhelming tenure approval Finkelstein had received at both the departmental and college levels. Finkelstein's scholarly work has accused Jewish groups of exploiting the Holocaust and Israel of egregious human rights violations. He had incurred the special wrath of Harvard law professor Alan Dershowitz, whose book defending Israel Finkelstein had devoted an entire book to savaging. Dershowitz, in turn, tried unsuccessfully to prevent the University of California Press from publishing Finkelstein's book, and sent Finkelstein's tenure committees a dossier that he said documented his "most egregious academic sins, and especially his outright lies, misquotations, and distortions." Clearly, the tenure committees were not impressed by Dershowitz's claims. DePaul president Dennis Holtschneider, for his part, denied that Dershowitz's intervention affected his decision.

Beshara Doumani, a University of California history professor, has mapped the systemic strategy of the New McCarthyism, highlighting that more than just its targets are new. First and foremost, private advocacy groups, not Congressional committees, are by and large today's means of pressuring academic administrations—at least, so far. These groups often retain important ties to government figures. But they are most focused on organizing alumni and students, with an eye toward generating public outrage and eventually government and donor pressure.

"I'm worried about untenured professors trying to get tenure," said Doumani, co-chair of the Middle East Studies Association's Committee on Academic Freedom. "I'm worried about entire departments saying, 'We need people in Middle East positions, but we're not going to hire certain kinds of people. It involves too much headache, too much risk.' How do you quantify that? You can't. But it's going around. I can tell you, it's a real issue."

Skeptics Are Denied Freedom of Expression on the Subject of Climate Change

Peter Lilley

Peter Lilley is a Conservative Party member of the British Parliament.

In the following selection, Lilley defends the skeptical view of climate change and its devastating effects on humanity. He cites other anticipated events that never came to pass—such as the year 2000 software meltdown and the discovery of weapons of mass destruction in Iraq—for which the alleged expert consensus led to costly and dangerous preparations. Lilley blames the "groupthink" phenomenon for blinding individuals to critical thought when there is overwhelming publicity that supports an argument such as climate change. When dissent is all but criminalized, Lilley contends, the checks and balances that otherwise protect democracy are undermined and the negative effects of climate change legislation are ignored until it is too late.

It is easy to mock the thousands of activists, officials and ministers flying to Copenhagen [Denmark, in 2009 for the United Nations Climate Change Conference] in their jets, driving around in an immense fleet of limousines, and collectively emitting more carbon dioxide than a small African country—all to force the rest of us to reduce our carbon footprints. But it is one thing to accuse them of hypocrisy in not living out their beliefs. Casting doubt on their belief that global warming poses an imminent threat to life on this planet is another.

To question so much scientific expertise and governmental authority seems arrogant or foolhardy—even in the city where Hans Christian Anderson wrote about the little boy who blurted out that the Emperor had no clothes.

When "Consensus" Becomes Truth

Can so many experts be wrong? Well, it is worth remembering that the experts were supposedly united about the apocalyptic dangers of the Y2K millennium bug. Half the world was persuaded to spend an estimated $600 billion to save us from disasters that embarrassingly failed to materialize in the countries and companies that omitted to take any pre-emptive action. Then intelligence agencies around the world were allegedly so convinced that [Iraqi dictator] Saddam Hussein had weapons of mass destruction that we went to war, only to find—zilch. In both cases there was a solid foundation of truth on which enthusiastic professionals and governments constructed an exaggerated scare story that the media lapped up. I was skeptical enough to delve into both those scares and rapidly found the experts were not as unanimous as supposed. But the dissenters were persuaded to keep quiet, bar a handful who were ruthlessly stereotyped as mavericks or worse.

In each case the driving force was "groupthink." [Psychologist] Irving Janis defined this as "a mode of thinking that people engage in when they are deeply involved in a cohesive in-group, when the members' strivings for unanimity override their motivation to realistically appraise alternative courses of action." The symptoms include:

> "Unquestioned belief in the morality of the group; Stereotyping those who are opposed to the group as evil, biased, etc.; Direct pressure to conform placed on any member who questions the group; Self-censorship of ideas that deviate from the apparent group consensus; Illusions of unanimity among group members, silence is viewed as agreement."

Campaigners against climate change show remarkably similar symptoms. . . .

The tendency of those committed to the theory of catastrophic man-made global warming to unquestioningly adopt the assumptions, at every stage, that maximize the expectation of calamity should alert us that groupthink is driving the movement.

The recently leaked email exchanges between scientists at the Climatic Research Unit in East Anglia and their colleagues in the U.S., who are among the illuminati of the global warming movement, show vivid evidence of groupthink at work. These scientists have become so committed to a cause that they think it natural to perform "tricks" to "hide the decline," as one email says. Another is so upset by "The fact . . . that we can't account for the lack of warming at the moment and it is a travesty that we can't" that he suggests "the data are surely wrong." It is reminiscent of the German philosopher [Georg W.F.] Hegel who, on being told by his disciples that the facts refuted his scientific theories, replied: "So much the worse for the facts." It is clear that while governments think they are pursuing evidence-based policies, these institutes have been serving up "policy-based evidence."

Criticism Excluded from the Debate

The whole U.N. Intergovernmental Panel on Climate Change process could not be better designed to institutionalize groupthink on a global scale. It puts enthusiasts at the helm. It seeks to establish a single view on the science, modeling, and economics. Dissent is banished. Loyalty is demanded. Silence is deemed consent. Moral fervor is reinforced by massive cash research budgets.

Even the British parliament has become caught up in groupthink. Dissent (and there are silent skeptics in both Labour and Conservative ranks) is suppressed by equating skepticism with Holocaust denial. Moral zeal replaces reasoned debate. Scrutiny of costs and benefits of alternative policy options is suspended. Desirable policies such as nuclear power to reduce dependency on hydrocarbons are sidelined in favor of a whimsical dependency on wind and sunshine.

When the Climate Change Bill passed through parliament [in 2008], I read the cost benefit assessment ministers are obliged to produce for any bill. Amazingly, it put the potential costs (of reducing carbon emissions by 60%) at £205 billion ($331 billion)—yet the maximum benefits (of reduced climate change damage) were estimated at only £110 billion. This is the first time any government had asked parliament to support a bill that its own figures say will do more harm than good. Yet just five of us voted against it. At least I had the satisfaction of pointing out that while the House was voting for a bill based on the assumption the world is getting warmer, it was snowing in London in October for the first time in 74 years. I was told, "extreme cold is a symptom of man made global warming."

The absurdity did not end there. Because the target for reducing emissions was amended upwards to 80%, I asked for a new cost-benefit assessment. Ministers eventually slipped one out—long after the bill had become an Act. It showed that the cost of meeting this more onerous target had doubled to £400 billion. Yet, miraculously, the government estimate of the likely benefits had risen tenfold. They had apparently previously mislaid nearly £1 trillion of benefits. It would be hard to find clearer evidence of the flaky nature of figures governments employ to justify their commitment to climate-change policies.

More carried away by groupthink than his colleagues, [British prime minister] Gordon Brown has strutted his stuff in Copenhagen—the prime minister of a near-bankrupt country offering to bankroll a global deal. When he returns we will find that although the benefits are flaky, the costs are real.

For Further Discussion

1. In Christopher Meeks' interview with Jerome Lawrence and Robert Edwin Lee in Chapter 1, Lawrence states: "Every playwright must have *creative* memory. You take your past and personal history, and stick to it literally, but there's no such thing as literal history. You have the obligation to be creative with personal memory and with history." Yet many critics find fault with historical plays that twist factual truths. In Chapter 2, Carol Iannone, in particular, argues that the play's distortion of historical truth has been damaging. What do the other selections in Chapter 2 say about this distortion of truth in the play? Which of these selections defend *Inherit the Wind*'s distortion of history? Why do they defend it? Do you believe distorting historical truth in fiction can be damaging? Why or why not?

2. In Chapter 2, Kay Cattarulla explains that premiering *Inherit the Wind* in Dallas was a risk, but that in the end it led the play to great success. Why was premiering in Dallas risky? If the play premiered in Dallas today, do you think it would have similar success? Why or why not? How do you think Mark Lawson (Chapter 2) would answer this question?

3. In Chapter 2, Gad Guterman states: "As the Christian Right has strengthened its political activism and successfully championed an accompanying cultural upheaval, the role of *Inherit the Wind* within the debate over evolution has changed and continues to change." Do you believe there has been a "cultural upheaval" in society caused by the Christian Right? Why or why not?

4. In Chapter 2, Phillip E. Johnson ends his article with the story of fifteen-year-old Danny Phillips, who argued against the showing of a television program espousing evolution in his school and lost. Johnson compares Phillips with *Inherit the Wind*'s character Bert Cates, even though the two represent opposite sides of the evolution debate. Do you see similarities between Danny Phillips and Bert Cates? Why or why not? How does the theme of 'freedom of thought' fit into this question? How do you think Edward J. Larson (Chapter 2) would respond to this comparison? What kinds of differences do you think he might point out?

5. The issue of evolution in the classroom has become a heated debate involving students, teachers, school boards, administrators, and parents and has regularly entered the political arena and the courthouse. In Chapter 3, the viewpoints of Jean Morse-Chevrier and David Postman detail stories of religion in the classroom being debated in courts. How do these modern stories compare/contrast with the court case depicted in *Inherit the Wind*?

For Further Reading

Jerome Lawrence and Robert E. Lee, *Auntie Mame*. New York: Vanguard Press, 1957.

————, *A Call on Kuprin*. New York: Samuel French, 1961.

————, *First Monday in October*. New York: Samuel French, 1979.

————, *The Gang's All Here*. Cleveland: World, 1960.

————, *The Incomparable Max*. New York: Dramatist's Play Service, 1972.

————, *Jabberwock: Improbabilities Lived and Imagined by James Thurber in the Fictional City of Columbus, Ohio*. New York: Samuel French, 1974.

————, *Mame*. New York: Random House, 1967.

————, *The Night Thoreau Spent in Jail*. New York: Hill & Wang, 1971.

————, *Only in America*. New York: Samuel French, 1960.

————, *Sparks Fly Upward*. New York: Dramatist's Play Service, 1967.

Bibliography

Books

Terry Chistner — *God vs. Darwin: The War Between Evolution and Creationism in the Classroom.* Lanham, MD: Rowman & Littlefield, 2009.

Richard L. Coe — "Jerome Lawrence," in *The Playwright's Art: Conversations with Contemporary American Dramatists.* Piscataway, NJ: Rutgers University Press, 1995.

Sean Connolly — *Religious Freedom.* Mankato, MN: Smart Apple Media, 2005.

Richard Dawkins — *The Greatest Show on Earth: The Evidence for Evolution.* New York: Free Press, 2009.

David Edwards — *Burning All Illusions: A Guide to Personal and Political Freedom.* Cambridge, MA: South End Press, 1999.

Stephanie Fitzgerald — *McCarthyism: The Red Scare.* Mankato, MN: Compass Point Books, 2006.

James Cross Giblin — *The Rise and Fall of Senator Joe McCarthy.* New York: Clarion Books, 1996.

| Anthony Lewis | *Freedom for the Thought That We Hate: A Biography of the First Amendment.* Jackson, TN: Basic Books, 2010. |

| Leonard Maltin | *The Great American Broadcast.* New York: New American Library Trade, 2000. |

| Kenneth McIntosh and Marsha McIntosh | *Issues of Church, State, and Religious Liberties.* Broomall, PA: Mason Crest, 2005. |

| Rebecca Stefoff | *Charles Darwin and the Evolution Revolution.* New York: Oxford University Press, 1996. |

Periodicals

| Austin Dacey | "Evolution in the Limelight," *Skeptical Inquirer*, September/October 2007. |

| Rob Davies | "Why Genesis and Darwin DO Match," *Daily Post* (Liverpool, UK), December 26, 2009. www.thefreelibrary.com. |

| Richard Dawkins | "The Angry Evolutionist," *Newsweek*, October 5, 2009. |

| Chuck Hagel | "Why Democracy Matters," *USA Today*, January 2009. |

| Corey Kilgannon | "Origin of the Species, from an Alien View," *New York Times*, January 10, 2010. |

Susan King — "The Blacklist's Gray Tones," *Los Angeles Times*, August 31, 2003.

John Leonard — "The Myth of Evolution," *Right Side News*, January 1, 2010.

James McKinley Jr. — "Split Outcome in Texas Battle on Teaching of Evolution," *New York Times*, January 23, 2009.

Randy Moore — "The Lingering Impact of *Inherit the Wind*," *American Biology Teacher*, April 1999.

Robert Price — "Apex or Ex-ape?" *Humanist*, January/February 2010.

Matthew J. Tontonoz — "The Scopes Trial Revisited: Social Darwinism Versus Social Gospel," *Science as Culture*, June 2008.

Internet Sources

William Saletan — "What Matters in Kansas: The Evolution of Creationism," *Slate*, May 11, 2005. www.slate.com/id/2118320.

Gordy Slack — "The Evolution of Creationism," *Salon*, November 13, 2007. www.salon.com/news/feature/2007/11/13/intelligent_design.

Index